UNDER THE BRIDGE

UNDER THE BRIDGE

ROBIN ARMSTRONG

GEORGE
PHILIP

For Tricia

ACKNOWLEDGEMENTS

I should like to thank the following people for their help in preparing this book. John Gaisford and Nigel Flynn, for patiently editing the script; Garry Metters, John Dodd, Brummie Cole, the late John Ainsworth, and many other 'men of the rivers', without whom the stories would hold no truth; John Kelley (for the jacket photograph); the old South West Water Authority, for giving me the chance and reason to recount my final year; and finally and above all – Bob Speddy.

Published by George Philip Limited,
59 Grosvenor Street, London W1X 9DA

British Library Cataloguing in Publication Data

Armstrong, Robin
 Under the bridge.
 I. Title
 344.10376921
ISBN 0-540-01246-7

Page design Gwyn Lewis
Typeset by Keyspools Limited, Golborne, Lancashire, Great Britain
Printed in Hong Kong

TITLE-PAGE ILLUSTRATION
Hiding among the roots of an alder, this fine salmon is about to fall victim to the poacher's snare

CONTENTS

PREFACE

U*nder the Bridge* follows on from two earlier books, *The Painted Stream* and *Split-Cane and Sable*, in describing something of my days as a water bailiff, wildlife artist and fisherman on the western fringes of Dartmoor.

Since the publication of *Split-Cane and Sable* and after some argument, I ceased to work for the old South West Water Authority. As my parting with the Authority is of general rather than merely personal interest, I have included an account of it in my introduction. This book, however, is only in very small part about my dealings with a now disbanded bureaucracy; its real origins lie in the days when I was contentedly doing my job as a water bailiff and painting in my spare time.

Between March 1988 and February 1989 I wrote a series of articles about the day-to-day life of a West Country river warden which were published in the magazine *Salmon, Trout and Sea Trout*. Based on my own experiences, these articles succeeded in arousing some interest and garnering some praise. At various times it was suggested to me that I ought to make them into a book. I hesitated before agreeing to do this. After all, what I had described in these articles related to conditions prevailing some time ago, and I felt that things might have changed since then. But I was assured that I need not worry; trout and salmon come and go in timeless patterns and water bailiffs continue to face the same problems as those I had experienced; my thoughts would still be relevant. More importantly, a book would give me the chance to develop my views on conservation and the prospects for our rivers at rather greater

OPPOSITE
A motor-cycle stands hidden behind a gate — ready for a poacher's getaway?

length and with more continuity than the articles permitted.

And so I came to write this book—altered a bit from the original articles, expanded and amended in places, rethought and in part rewritten, but still based on actual events. If at times I have added colour to lighten the reading, or ascribed fictitious names to certain people to avoid contention, I have never done so at the expense of underlying truth. This is a true account of the job a water bailiff in West Devon was expected to do, the sort of year I could expect to face, the pattern of my seasonal life and the fears and hopes I have about the future of the wild and lovely countryside in which I live and work.

In the field and the laboratory—if not always in parts of Head Office—the Water Authority introduced me to a rewarding number of skilled and helpful colleagues with whom it was a pleasure and a privilege to work. They do important jobs, relatively unnoticed, and it is to them that I dedicate this book.

NOTE

The various names given to trout, salmon and sea trout at different stages of their life-cycles are:

ALEVIN   Generic term for any young fish but usually applied to young salmon and trout.

FRY   Young fish newly spawned.

GRILSE   A young salmon on its first return from the sea to the river for spawning.

KELT   A salmon or sea trout after spawning.

PARR/PAR   A young salmon in the early stages of its river life.

PEAL   The West Country name for a sea trout; a small sea trout.

REDD   Gravel shallows on which salmon and trout spawn.

SMOLT   A young salmon or sea trout in an intermediate state between parr and grilse, just ready to migrate to the sea for the first time.

INTRODUCTION

I first became a water bailiff on an honorary basis in the early 1970s. I had come to West Devon because I loved its wild moors and rivers and was attracted by the idea of living outside the constraints of nine-to-five office hours in someone else's service. I would become, I thought, a full-time, wildlife artist; self-sufficient and beholden to no one.

I was fooling myself. No man is an island, and I am no ascetic. There are times when I love being alone, but there are also times when I need company. I could live without luxury, but I did need more money than I was then earning. My paintings at the time brought in less than enough for civilized life and I had not then acquired the discipline needed to make a proper living from artistic self-employment. Spending almost as many hours on the river and in the pub as I was in my studio, when I was offered a full-time, permanent and pensionable post with South West Water Authority, I decided to take it. I knew I would enjoy the work and the chances it would give me to learn more about fishing and wildlife, while the security provided by a regular wage would allow me, I thought, to approach my painting with greater serenity. I would be paid for doing what I was already doing for love and I would be forced by the demands of full-time work to organize my time more productively. The busier one is, the more one finds space to do further things.

I never regretted the decision. Working as a bailiff, or more correctly a river warden, taught me more about rivers and wild-life than I could ever have learned from books or from fishing. It also taught me much about people, for fishermen, legitimate and illegitimate, encompass a wide cross-section of humanity. I met anglers of every sort and social class, pleasant and unpleasant. I dealt with poachers with whom I felt a sneaking rapport, and poachers whom I detested. I worked with colleagues whom I greatly respected and some superiors whom I held in contempt. And I made many friends who still enrich my present life and my memories.

Izaak Walton's beloved 'brotherhood of the angle' does not always extend to bailiffs, and there were still a few fishermen—often those richer in tackle than technique—who believed that their dues bought them the bailiff's servility. On the river bank, the curse of the English caste-system has not everywhere been exorcized. But for the most part, people were prepared to listen and follow the rules. In my twelve years as a water bailiff, I made many more good friends than enemies. I am prejudiced, perhaps, but my West Country experience is that most anglers are decent and civilized folk; much more deeply-versed in the mysteries of their chosen craft than many followers of other sports and less inclined to envy others' success.

Looking back, my move into one of the oldest of country trades must have been dictated by fate, or sprung from some long dormant gene, since it was certainly not fostered in me by my immediate family, none of whom knew one end of a fishing rod from the other. I had not been brought up in rural surroundings and no one had ever consciously encouraged me to take up rural pursuits, at least not until after I had developed my own interest in fishing at the age of seven in the unlikely waters of Finsbury Park pond—a long time ago and a long way, in distance and culture, from the Devon valley where I now live.

Finsbury Park fish were very different from the carefree trout and salmon which grace the stream below the cottage in which I now live. They were mostly tired perch, stunted in growth, with lungs blackened by urban dirt and natures made cynical by deprivation. They lived mainly, I suspect, on breadcrumbs thrown to them by children whose place in the human pecking order matched theirs in the domain of fish. They were not, in short, much sought after by anglers of the first class. We who

hunted them were mainly small boys or shabby old men made
redundant or retired from whatever wretched positions, if any,
they had once held. Our rods were home-made, our baits were
whatever we could spare from our packed lunches and our creels
were old shopping bags, much worn. On the rare occasions when
one of us caught anything, all activity on the bedraggled bankside
would cease, as fellow anglers crowded round to admire the puny
trophy—usually so small that it had to be thrown back.

That, I suppose, was fishing at its most primitive, as far
removed from an expensive day on a salmon river as it is possible
to find. But it was fishing and we loved it. Even if our
surroundings were far from bucolic; even if the bird-song was
limited to the shrieks of careless starlings, taken by cats too poor
to have known the joys of expensive tinned food; even if we spent
anxious moments walking home past a tide of drunken vagrants—
we still thought it worthwhile. Nothing, in our urchin minds,

My cottage in West Devon

could compare with matching wits against a city-bred perch. Since we had no experience of other fishing, our judgement was perhaps somewhat biased.

Early childhood passed quickly. Soon I began to try other ponds and new rivers and the sea—experiences which I have already recorded in *Split-Cane and Sable*. It was an enjoyable and productive apprenticeship. During its course, I learned much about every sort of fish and fishing, soaked up knowledge of birds and plant life and became thoroughly conversant with country ways. But I was certainly not consciously seeking to equip myself for work as a river warden, even though that indeed was what I was doing. It was only later I realized the value of that self-taught groundwork, even though, after my first patrols, it soon became obvious that there was still a lot more to learn about my new rivers, the ways of the fish in them and the habits of those who tried to lift the fish illegally. Twenty years on, I must wryly acknowledge that I am still learning.

Most of my time with South West Water Authority was spent in West Devon covering Dartmoor and the great estuaries of the Plym and the Tamar. Occasionally I was given tasks in East and North Devon and in Cornwall, but it was the Walkham and Tavy rivers, and the small streams of the high moor which fed them, with which I was most concerned. It was wonderful country in which to work. Rich in the variety of its scenery and changing moods, it combines hard, stern moorland, soft fields and woods. To the north, granite tors rise above uncultivated valleys, while nearer the estuaries of the Dart and Tamar, the scenery is gentler and more domesticated. The rivers, too, are changeable and volatile—heavy rain on the high moor runs off the harsh hillsides and rushes down the valleys very quickly, transforming the water overnight. One day a river is bright and clear; the next it becomes a raging torrent of swirling brown water, impossible to fish. Always, though, it retains its enchantment, for there is something about running water which appeals to the primitive in all of us.

I did not have to work for very long as a warden to realize how very lucky I was. I had escaped the nine-to-five routine of commuter trains and week upon week of similar papers facing me at the same daily desk. My hours were erratic, the tasks I was called

OPPOSITE
Fishing in the river in springtime

upon to do changed with the seasons. Every month was different and even during those weeks when I was doing the same daily patrol, I was not usually confined to one location, but moving about from place to place, rebuilding old friendships and making new ones. Variety, in short, is the essence of the warden's life, and I enjoyed it. Had I been a private bailiff in earlier times, working for one master and stolidly treading the same stretch of river bank every day with little more to do than warn off some known poachers, or occasionally restock with hatched fish, I might have become bored. My job was much more positive than that—my responsibilities were wider, my work led me to fast patrol boat chases on the estuaries one day, followed by high-technology research the next, with a myriad different duties in between.

My job also allowed me to mix with a more disparate and interesting band of colleagues than I would have found on the river bank in earlier days. By the time I joined the Water Authority, the old image of the bailiff as a rustic heavy with a big dog and a thick stick was no longer appropriate. We still needed some physical presence, for many of the poachers and potential poachers with whom we dealt were violent men, but that alone was insufficient qualification for the new breed of river warden. If we were not ourselves qualified scientists, we at least had to understand the nature of science and have sympathy with scientific methods. If we were not trained administrators, we at least had to know how to keep proper records and write reports. If we were not trained psychologists, we at least had to know how to handle people. If we were not policemen, we at least had to be able to follow the rules of evidence and criminal procedures well enough to win cases.

We were a diverse group, not easy to classify. Sitting in a pub, I doubt if we looked any different from anyone else. We came in all physical shapes and intellectual sizes, most of which were far removed from accepted stereotypes. We had quiet men and noisy men, doers and thinkers, sons of the soil and sons of towns. We had one ex-SAS man, small, tough and much inclined to the physical solution of all disputes. We had ex-seamen, a graduate or two and, in the later years of my service, a woman—one of the first ever to be appointed. All of these people held widely differing

Sea trout fly

views on most subjects, but all shared a love of the countryside and a knowledge of the rivers for which we were responsible. We knew that to achieve good results against poachers or polluters we had to work as a team, and by and large, we did so, successfully and amicably, cherishing the same sort of pride as members of a football squad or soldiers in the same regiment. I confess, too, that we felt a healthy superiority over those clerks who ruled over us from the comfort of a warm office. We were the Authority's front-line men, the ones on the ground, close to the real world and in direct contact with the owners and anglers whom we served.

By March 1989, I had been a bailiff for some eleven years — fourteen altogether, if my previous honorary, part-time work was counted. I had enjoyed the job and got along well with colleagues with whom I shared watch along river bank and shoreline. But I was never the favourite of my superiors and I knew, subconsciously, that sooner or later we were bound to fall out. The thought was not a happy one, for after all, the Authority provided me with security and the opportunity to travel about some of the loveliest rivers in England. It paid me for doing what I enjoyed doing and gave me the chance to improve my knowledge of riverine flora and fauna. It even smoothed my way to fish. When I finally left the Authority's employ, therefore, I did so with a somewhat tremulous heart.

The security of an assured monthly salary cheque disappeared. The discipline imposed by paid employment — having to go to work by a certain hour on certain days, having to do whatever task was set by the Authority — also went. In order to eat, I had to re-learn the art of self-motivation and how to schedule my working life to that of a full-time artist. While I was working for the Water Authority I painted only when the fancy took me, picking my subjects from things I had done or seen on duty. My work and my painting in some ways went hand in hand. There was no immediate financial pressure on me to paint to order. Now, however, I had to recognize that I would need to watch my finances rather more carefully than in the past, for if I fell sick, there would be no sick pay; if I went on holiday, my income would cease, and if I survived into old age, there would be no pension, except that which I had personally arranged.

Why, then, did I part company with what in many respects was a fair and benevolent employer? South West Water Authority was not noticeably mean, nor excessive in the demands it made on its employees, and for the most part it treated us reasonably. Bailiffs were provided with every aid and comfort to carry out their work. We had 'Barbour' jackets, not cheap imitations; we had the very best binoculars, rather than perfectly serviceable but cheaper ones made in the Far East at a sixth of the price (one man lost three pairs in the course of a year); we had generous car allowances and few people were ever disciplined for misconduct or lack of application. For myself, I had already had more than one letter commending me for good work. It was therefore a shock when, in March 1988, I was called to the Area Office to discuss 'allegations of misconduct'.

These 'allegations' were not presented as formal charges under the Authority's disciplinary procedures, and their exact nature was never made clear to me. In brief, however, I was said to have 'written books and articles' and to have 'spoken to the media without permission of the Authority'; to have 'made sketches in notebooks' and to have 'failed to hand in certain notebooks' to the office.

The 'charges' were not matters of life or death, but they worried me. I could have answered them all easily without having to visit the office and undergo a 'hearing', which, when it occurred, did not even follow the Authority's own strict rules governing such a procedure. Why was I being asked to account for making sketches in notebooks when I had already submitted them to the Authority years before? It seemed to me that some unknown senior official was after my blood. But for what reason?

The 'allegations' or 'charges'—I was not quite sure of their exact status—were, in my view, absurd. My first book, *The Painted Stream*, had been published some three years previously and had received praise from a senior manager of South West Water Authority. The same official had known that the book would attract publicity and that I would be interviewed by the media. Not only had he accepted that, but he had hinted that I might be of

OPPOSITE
An inquisitive otter alongside the river

use to the Authority in a public relations role. I therefore assumed, with good reason, that my writing and painting was welcomed by the Authority. Not only did I not write anything critical of the Authority, but the few references I made to it were full of praise for its good work in pollution control and enforcement. In any case, if I had wanted to criticize the Authority I would have submitted such criticisms to my boss and not have aired them in public.

I was, however, guilty of one piece of lese-majesty. In *Split-Cane and Sable* I had drawn a picture of a cormorant next to a broken wooden notice which declared that 'Trespassers will be shot'. It was signed—in letters illegible except through a magnifying glass—by an unyielding manager from whom I, like many others, had often suffered minor admonitions. It was a joke, a piece of foolery which, although perhaps not quite fair, had never been mentioned before. Could it be that no one had noticed it until now?

The first interview I had with my superiors was inconclusive. I was left not knowing if they intended to go any further with their 'allegations' or whether they merely wished to issue some form of warning along the lines of: 'Watch your step, Armstrong'. On reflection, I thought that their action might perhaps have been prompted by envy. My books and paintings had attracted a lot of attention and had led to my mixing with and getting to know on first-name terms many riparian owners. Was it this that my masters disliked? In the country, caste and class jealousies remain powerful forces.

For six months I lived under the threat of disciplinary action being taken against me by the Authority. No matter how absurd the 'allegations', they clearly signalled some senior's animosity towards me. As there had been no mention of my being suspended, I continued to work as best I could. But the uncertainty became intolerable and I found it increasingly difficult to ignore the threat hanging over me. Under the weight of unfair suspicion I almost broke down and was totally unable to paint. Then, in August 1988, I received a letter from the Authority in which they restated their previous allegations and added another—that I had 'fished without a licence in the area of another

A pied flycatcher in action

Water Authority', thereby (presumably) bringing discredit on my own.

The facts concerning all the 'allegations' made against me were simple and straightforward. As a fairly well-known local artist I had attracted the interest of the Devon media for some ten years. The Authority knew of this and had never told me that I was not allowed to comment on my own work. No one had ever suggested that I submit my work to the Authority for their approval before selling it. On the contrary, a senior manager had actually congratulated me on my efforts. As to the charge that I had used official notebooks for my drawings and had not returned them to the Authority, I would have to plead guilty. But I had been drawing birds and animals and little maps to remind me of what I had seen for years, and with the knowledge of my supervisor. As to my not returning my notebooks, I saw no need to do so as they had already been checked by the Authority and were now safely stored in a loft.

But these were trivial issues which, if I were thicker-skinned, I could have dismissed with contempt or put aside without a second thought. The charge of fishing without a licence was an altogether different matter—more serious and potentially damaging both to my professional and my personal reputation. Even from this distance in time, as it was so ludicrous, it annoys me to think of it.

The circumstances which led to this accusation were straight-forward. I had been fishing a Hampshire chalk stream at the invitation of an eminent Hampshire fisherman—a man who was president of his country-wide, professional association and well-known in the club to which he had introduced me as his guest. When I was approached by a river warden and asked to produce my licence, I replied cheerfully that I was the guest of 'Mr X', who could be found further upstream and who would vouch for me. After I had revealed that I too was a bailiff, and having exchanged a few pleasantries about the nature of our respective jobs in Hampshire and Devon, the warden moved off to find my friend.

It was to prove a bad day for me. My friend—rich, respected and normally highly responsible—had forgotten to renew his licence. It was out of date. We were both breaking the law, even if I had made a genuine, and as my eminent friend explained to the Bench, understandable mistake for which he took responsibility. But the law admitted of no exceptions; this was an offence which if proved or admitted meant that the defendant must be found guilty. Mitigating circumstances can only be taken into account in sentencing. The best the Court could do for me, which it did, was to give me an 'absolute discharge'—the equivalent of saying that a technical offence had been committed, but that the Court effectively exonerated me from any criminal intent.

I was entirely at fault in not checking my friend's licence before I began to fish, but it was hardly surprising that I failed to do so, and I suspect that most people in the same position would have been equally remiss. Given the proven circumstances, I found it strange that the matter was taken as far as a prosecution, but even stranger that my masters should want to add it to the list of accusations which faced me. I felt I was being hounded for no good reason, and I began to feel thoroughly unsettled and depressed—so much so that, for a time, I was unable to work. In the end, I finally left the Water Authority, recompensed with a gratuity and a pension, in May 1989. But the manner of my going was not that which I would have chosen.

Why relate this tale? Because I think it shows how a cosy, relatively unaccountable bureaucracy can act. I could have chosen to make much more fuss than I did, but no one wants to have his name splashed about local newspapers in connection with disciplinary proceedings—besides which the emotional and financial costs of defending oneself are not negligible. I was also fairly sure, after taking professional advice, that senior management could not have been aware of what was being perpetrated in their name. No company in the late 1980s could possibly have countenanced—at board level—the instigation of disciplinary proceedings against a staff member in such an ill-conceived way. The normal rules applying to such a hearing had been flouted, and there was a delay of six months between the first hearing and the Authority taking the matter up again with fresh accusations. To any impartial observer, the charges and proceedings would have appeared laughably inept and I was fairly certain that once the matter came to the attention of the board, my position would be vindicated. Meanwhile, to be on the receiving end of such distasteful comings and goings was both disturbing and upsetting.

Over the years I worked for South West Water, the number of pollution incidents rose sharply, and the dangers from a deliberate or accidental discharge of farm slurry, chemicals and sewage became increasingly obvious. The carelessness of a single farmer or plant operative could destroy thousands of fish in a single night. Nor was the Water Authority itself above error. On more than one occasion the River Tavy was harmed by the release of excessive domestic sewage into a river system that could not absorb it. The old Authority failed too, I think, in not prosecuting a more determined anti-pollution policy. Fish killed by 'accidental' discharges of slurry might have been saved had the Authority acted more vigorously in prosecuting the culprits in previous cases. With pollution of this kind, declining numbers of salmon and sea trout entering the estuaries, and poachers becoming more numerous and better equipped to outsmart the bailiffs who seek to catch them, game fishing faces a very uncertain future.

Happily, not all the trends are regressive. In the past few years the good has begun to overtake the bad, or at least, to catch up with it. Public, press and politicians have become more interested in conservation and more prepared to pay the cost. Our rivers are again seen as a precious asset rather than as convenient dumping grounds. Long before privatization, Water Authorities had begun to acknowledge the need to employ more and better qualified staff to supervise and advance their ecological, enforcement and recreational responsibilities, while more money was being put into staff training and research. In the case of South West Water, I certainly felt that conditions of employment and the facilities offered to the public on the rivers and lakes under our charge were steadily improving.

But I do not see that we can be complacent. For every three steps forward, international fishermen, local polluters and poachers can very quickly drag us two steps back. The threat to salmon starts with professional overfishing in the far North Atlantic—difficult to control without complex international agreements—and continues on the estuaries and rivers to which they return in this country. In the relatively sparsely populated South West, our rivers face fewer threats from gravel workings and excessive nitrates than the chalk streams further east, but slurry remains a problem, and rising numbers of residents and tourists are making demands on our water resources unimagined a generation ago. The job of the bailiff is therefore more important than ever, for whatever research is done, or whatever laws are passed, someone has to be on daily guard on the river bank, watching fish, keeping an eye open for poachers and pollution and noting any depredations caused by storm and flood. Even the most sophisticated electronic device can never replace the man on the ground.

Here then, in the chapters that follow, is a description of what one man on the ground actually did in one particular part of the south west of England. The bailiff's job elsewhere in the country might differ in the emphasis placed on certain aspects of his daily round, but the job itself is broadly the same everywhere—improving the quality of our rivers, making them better places for fish, protecting fish stocks against poachers and pollution and safeguarding their long-term future. It was, and is, a worthwhile job which will need to be done so long as we have rivers and angling continues as a major sport. I certainly enjoyed doing it and so, despite grumbles about having to work at awkward times in all sorts of weather, did most of my colleagues. Whether bailiffing is a profession, a trade, or a vocation, I do not know. I do know that most of those who pursue it are men with a fairly deep understanding and sense of purpose of what they are doing. Any angler who wishes to improve his fishing technique could do worse than ask their advice—not many amateur river men will have studied the run of fish as carefully as a water bailiff.

Wild duck's nest, complete with eggs

CHAPTER ONE

SWALLOWS AND ALEVINS

A swallow chasing flies in springtime

March comes to West Devon like an inconstant mistress, fickle and unpredictable; splashing bright sunshine on to green fields one day, and whitening them with snow the next. This is the month when prevailing balmy south-westerlies may turn into freezing east winds overnight, causing the first of the returning swallows to complain testily that British weather is not what it was, and to curse themselves for volunteering to be the pathfinders. This, according to Chaucer, is the 'month when the world began, and God first maked man'; the time for the game fishing season to open and for the first cautious alevins to stir from their chilly redds. This, in brief, is the time when water bailiffs up and down the country celebrate, or curse, the true beginnings of their working year.

On Dartmoor, this boisterous month also brings sight of the first well-wrapped-up emmets and grockels, the tourists who see us variously as slow and quaint and olde worlde rustics, full of cream teas and rough cider. In total, some ten million visitors will be attracted to the moor over the next twelve months, enough to fill Wembley Stadium a hundred times, or populate Ireland twice over. And more than enough to put off even the most gregarious of anglers, let alone an average trout man, seeking no more than a few quiet hours of good sport on an exacting stream. I can already see fellow-fishermen making resolutions never to come near here, lest they find the rivers crowded with screaming children and paddlers in rolled-up trousers, with knotted handkerchiefs over their heads.

Faint hearts should fear not. The figures are deceptive, since they include every man, wife and mother-in-law whose weekend drives out from the surrounding towns bring them over the Tavistock-Ashburton road 'for the scenery'. Such day-trippers, along with most tourists, only stop in the National Park long enough to enjoy a cup of tea or an ice-cream before hastening back to their televisions. Relatively few of them ever leave the main highway and if they do, it is only to resist the lure of the distant tors, and to stretch their legs within a safe distance from their motor-cars.

Above and below the fringes of the roads, far from the motor-cars, coaches and madding crowds, was my territory. Before I begin to detail the seasonal work I did, perhaps I should describe the broad sweep of the country I worked in. In general, it is an area of ravishing emptiness, friendly enough in sunshine, but grim and menacing when the mists roll in and the clouds darken with impending rain. Its rivers are clean enough and largely unspoilt— so far; only if the bulk of tourists ever became more energetic and curious about what lies over the hills, would I fear for the future of our fishing grounds. But they do not. Half-a-mile up- or downstream from the roads and the chances are that you will see very few people. After a mile, you will almost certainly find yourself alone and free to fish to your heart's content. Only an occasional hiker; the melancholy cries of the curlews; the sounds of water tumbling over granite boulders and sheep baaing on the high hills and, if you are unlucky, a very distant noise of traffic, interrupts the silence. Dartmoor is happily still almost unspoilt. People make relatively few demands on its wilder parts, and fishermen—at least on the upland streams—can be pretty sure that the peaceful taking of small brown trout will not be interrupted by the thumping of transistors.

The moor was not my only stamping ground, but it was a big and much-loved part of it, and a lot of my bailiff's time was spent there. What can a serious trout fisherman expect to find on it?

Certainly not large rivers, as found in Scotland, nor waters brimming with suicidal fish. Here, we can only offer trout which have to be walked for and worked at. Over the high moor there are no gentle paths along the water's edge, nor pools big enough to provide a day's sport in one place. On the streams lying to the north of a line drawn between Grenofen and Ashburton, you must be prepared to move up and down and search for your fish fairly rigorously. And to do this, you must be lightly equipped and ready to face rugged conditions, for the water which yesterday was low and slow-moving could have turned by today into a raging torrent. You will need patience to work every inch of whatever water there is and the skill to winkle out your quarry once you think you have found him. Fish in this part of the world, made cunning by their harsh surroundings, lurk in the most unlikely refuges.

Lastly, but certainly not least of all, you will need the energy to climb over rocky outcrops and to skirt the bogs formed by water seeping down into the hillside re-entrants. West Devon boasts few shaven embankments and convenient footbridges; this is wilder country than you will find in Hampshire and the Home Counties and less angler-friendly. Here you must graft for your catch and be content if what you get from a day's work is less than a family panful. If all you want from fishing is to put in your hook and pull out a large rainbow, then turn your thoughts elsewhere.

Fly fishers do receive some encouragement from these stony waters. Where chalk-stream trout have lots to eat and are therefore not readily inclined to snatch at anything and everything that is offered to them, our trout are always hungry and less choosy. They may finally reject something, but they cannot afford to let it pass by without at least giving it a careful inspection. Thus anyone who can present a well-crafted fly with any degree of skill, can live in hope of some success—provided, of course, he has read the waters well and found fish in the first place.

The proviso is an important one. In my early years as a bailiff, when I first began walking these Dartmoor rivers as part of my work, I learned from Dartmoor characters like the late Bunny Spiller (of whom I have written elsewhere) that success here depended on meticulously working every nook, cranny, pot and

Vixen Tor   Robin Armstrong

sickle of every stream. Unfailingly courteous and immaculately turned out, he and his fellows of that generation never expected easy catches, nor would they have welcomed them. They enjoyed having to pit their wits against a wily quarry and their bodies against wild nature. They and their friends well knew that Dartmoor streams are not for fair-weather fishermen; they had seen too many bright mornings turn into wet, misty afternoons and they all accepted, with good natured stoicism, that the best of man's fishing plans may often be upset by sudden changes in weather and water.

Although a day's catch on Upper Dartmoor may not amount to much on the scales, it will certainly be worth eating. Valley fish may be fatter, but hill fish are sweeter. The products of our peaty

Vixen Tor looms above the River Walkham on the western edge of Dartmoor

streams may not be big, but they are beautiful. Firm-bodied and distinctive, they are the 'Jaguars' of the fish world, sleek and fast-moving, handsomely matched to their surroundings and supremely at home in the wild environment which the gods, or natural forces, have selected for them. It's as hard to imagine a flabby moor trout as it is to picture an out-of-condition Daley Thompson.

Visiting fishermen, accustomed to more gentle streams, would often ask me how to take fish from these waters, mistakenly imagining that as a bailiff I was possessed of secrets not open to other men. I would reply to an often sceptical listener that I did so with guile, persistence and, usually, a lightweight, split-cane rod; a two-pound cast and a local fly, probably a Half Stone. Or sometimes, the ever-favoured Gold Ribbed Hare's Ear, which the great F. M. Halford often used on the more placid waters of the Test, over a hundred years ago. But whatever the fly, none will be of any use until you can read the water and find your fish. And being able to do that, as 'Swifty' Warne, ex-bailiff and near genius of a fisherman used to tell me, 'needed a lot of learning'.

Wet fly

In the downstream parts of my erstwhile bailiwick, further south towards the sea, Dartmoor rivers assume a more conventional aspect and begin to look little different from those up-country. Soon after the swiftly flowing Tavy settles down to merge with the Walkham, its junior sibling, it becomes a fully paid-up member of the salmon, trout and sea trout rivers' association—the sort of river where respectable men in the right gear can be seen casting in the right way and pulling in respectable fish. And good luck to them; the conventional fishing presented in the lower reaches of all our rivers, including the lower reaches of the Tamar separating us from the Celtic wilds of Cornwall, is excellent.

None of our rivers, of course, is as placid nor as orderly as a chalk stream, except perhaps when their wayward falls are over and they are close to the sea. Even in those rivers like the Torridge and the Taw, where I occasionally worked, the gypsy influence of their beginnings on the high moor is always evident in their rapid rises and falls and changes of mood. But it is still possible to spend a day on the Walkham, below Grenofen, without exerting any more energy than you would on an artificial lake. Here, a dozen or so miles from the sea, the fish are as easy to take as any, especially in a dry summer when they congregate in a few known pools waiting to jostle upstream again to reach their spawning beds.

These, then, were the kind of rivers on which I worked; rural and mostly unspoilt, flowing much as they did fifty or more years ago, and still affording brown trout, salmon and sea trout—the fish with which I was mainly concerned—in some number. The trout are smaller than most (just over half a pound, compared with Test trout which average almost three times as much) and are better suited as a prelude to a good breakfast, than the main course of a heavy dinner. But they taste good and palates not ruined by city fumes might even detect a whiff of Dartmoor turf in them. Local fishermen, more chauvinistic than I, claim that our salmon and sea trout, which are rather smaller than those found on the big Scottish rivers, also have their own unique taste, and maybe they are right. I was certainly intrigued to discover that there are physical differences between the long, lean salmon—known locally as 'Tamar Greyhounds'—returning to the River Tamar, on the west side of the Tamar estuary, and the marginally plumper fish which choose to spawn in the River Tavy, only a few miles to the east. But even my practised artist's eye could not see anything between the fish going back to other rivers. I was content to view

Study of a toad

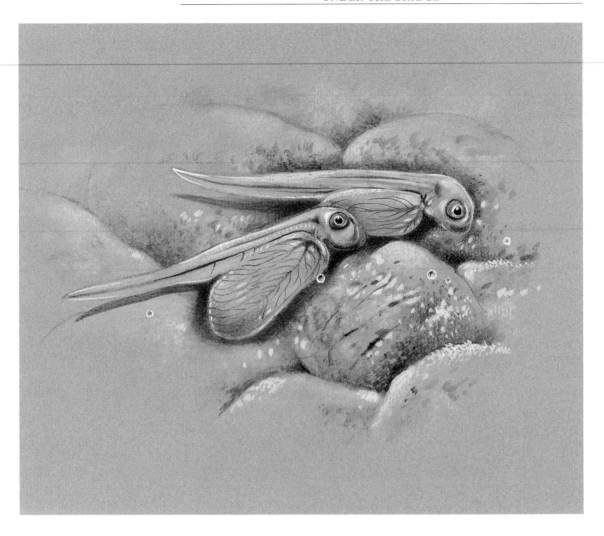

*A pair of alevins at rest
on the river bed*

them all as uniquely beautiful. If salmon must be weighed and measured and classified, and I suppose they must if we are to conserve them, then let others do the science while I rejoice in painting them.

Meanwhile, if those first March swallows were few and tentative, and their swoopings less exuberant than they would become when the main force arrived from Africa in mid-April, they were at least a firm reminder that a new season was already upon us; that the alevins, freshly spawned young fish, would soon be making their entrance into the wild world of the upper moor and that at any minute, a slumbering army of trout and salmon fishermen would wake to pester the nearest river keeper about prospects for the months to come. At this time of the year, everything is in a state of change. Spring—which on some country reckonings begins in February—brings back our West Country rivers to vivid life. By late April they are filling with darting smolt and lively 'springers', the first of the season's big fish, and their banks, at least in the urban parts, are crowding with small boys casting optimistically with Woolworths' rods and cheese-baited lines.

Their optimism will not be unfounded. Every so often, to the excited gasps of his friends, someone will land something worthwhile. The rest of us are then reassured that despite the fits and starts of the weather; despite economic crises, wars and rumours of wars, and foul contingency of every sort, we can be certain (almost) that Nature will always afford us another generous chance of a fresh start.

In its early weeks, when I used to rise in the cold dark, spring could be miserable. Whatever the official temperature, the Dartmoor chill factor lowers it. Climbing into my frozen car, slipping into four-wheel drive and steering gingerly up the snow-covered hill outside my house, I often wished that villains kept office hours. I knew in my bones that the sacrifice of a warm bed would only rarely lead to arrests. By the time I arrived at Grenofen Pool, the reported poachers would be long gone. Only about one in forty of the trips I made to investigate suspicious sightings ever produced results. By the time I arrived, the nefarious activity was usually over, and all I ever found were fresh tracks on the river bank or some newly discarded litter, which might mean lovers rather than criminals. The only satisfaction I used to get from my chilly rising was the knowledge that the poachers would certainly hear of it and take note. For them to know that I was sometimes abroad and wakeful at such an hour might just prove to be some small deterrent.

As with early spring weather, so with spring rivers. In West Devon they too are subject to rapid change, tonight's storm being predictably followed by tomorrow morning's floodwater. Rain is not absorbed as it is on the Wiltshire and Hampshire downs, to be released later, but pours off the granite tors very quickly, turning our rivers into rippling brown torrents through which fish sighting is almost impossible. On days like this I could only walk the banks and note, for report to headquarters, which overhangs were at risk from erosion; where a new ox-bow lake might be forming, and which weirs and bridges were endangered by tree branches brought down by the flood. The sight of an untamed spring river, swollen by heavy rain or melting snow, might have filled me with a sense of primitive energy and elation, but I well knew the damage which floodwater could do to cherished pools and overhangs. If changes were to be made to a river's course, I liked to dictate them myself, and not have them thrust upon me by the elements. The actual work of maintaining the banks, of course, was done by keepers, not by us. Our job was to deal directly with the public and perhaps even more importantly, the welfare of the fish. If, for example, the gravels of the spawning beds were washed away by a sudden flood, we would organize the building of steps to see that the salmon could swim further upriver into new water; if stocks became depleted by pollution, we would estimate the numbers needed to make up the deficiency from our hatchery at Endsleigh.

In the old days, Endsleigh was the hatchery of the Duke of Bedford, the nineteenth-century builder of Tavistock's town centre. However devoted his loyal servants, I doubt if they could have matched our expertise in the science of rearing fish; trapping hen salmon in the autumn, stripping them of their eggs, fertilizing them and keeping them for hatching in late February. Later, we would have to carry their young, known as parr, from hatchery to river in 500-gallon tanks on the precarious platform of a Land Rover. It was a tricky operation, having to gauge fairly carefully how many fish could be lifted without losing them for lack of oxygen, and having to drive such a weight of motor and trailer without mishap. It was certainly a sharp contrast to the more delicate work I was sometimes called to do as a relief in the clinically clean hatchery itself, learning the job as I went along and wishing my zoology was as advanced as that of our highly-skilled technicians.

The spring months of March through May were my time for

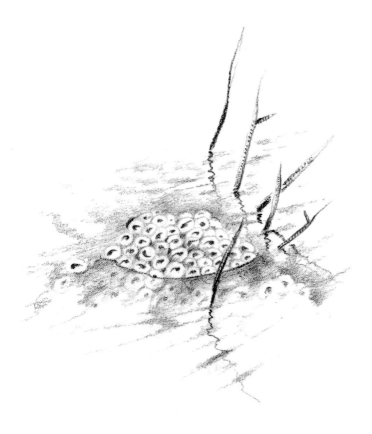

The arrival of spring is marked by the appearance of frog spawn

housekeeping—checking the state of the rivers and the movements of the new fish, and preparing my own personal gear for the busy days ahead. Some early days before the season got underway were spent repairing the boats and lakeside kiosks on our reservoirs at Fernworthy and Burrator; others were allocated to training sessions in which we were taught the mysteries of Fisheries legislation, and the need for accurate recording of what we did on enforcement duties. Mainly, though, routine 'OAPs'— organized anti-poaching patrols—occupied most of my early-year energies. Whatever else he does, a bailiff must walk his patch as often as he can so that he gets to know his rivers better than the anglers who fish them, and better than the poachers who steal from them. But it's no good his visiting each of the best reaches and pools in a predictable pattern. He must keep changing the times of his visits and the directions from which he makes them. He must also carefully note the numbers of suspiciously parked cars, memorize any new faces seen along the river bank, and keep an eye on the toing and froing of those whom he knows—but cannot prove—to be heavily involved in local poaching. Since the poachers themselves varied their routines as much as we did, it was never easy to predict where they might be at any given time.

But even the cleverest of villains may nod, and be as fallible as the rest of us. Some, dropping their customary guard, would occasionally work to routines that we could predict in advance. One local man, seized by the grip of habit, ignored the dog which didn't bark in the night—in this case the rabbit which failed to appear at the spot where he had seen it every morning for the past few days—and paid dearly for his lack of attention. When he failed to acknowledge the portent of the missing rabbit, and failed to sense that something was amiss in the early morning woods, our patrol, lying in wait where he had placed his net, was able to catch him red-handed when he came to examine his night's takings.

On that occasion we were successful; many other stake-outs were not, since poachers were normally more wary. But I still believed that preventative work was useful, and that painstaking observation, however tedious it was for the observers, did help to create a picture of the people we were up against and the methods they favoured. And however hard experienced poachers tried to avoid repeating themselves, it was inevitable that they sometimes did.

If good intelligence was essential to catching poachers, good intelligence, in a rural area, was mainly based on good liaison with the police; on meeting and talking to honest men, and some who were less than honest; on listening to pub gossip, while discounting most of it, and keeping a close eye on the changes in life-styles of those who openly boasted that their supplementary benefits derived in greater part from stolen fish than from the state. I would therefore spend some of my March days wandering about the edges of the Tamar estuary, talking to some of the legal netsmen on the one hand, and on the other noting who had bought new boats, nets and equipment which no honest amateur fisherman would need. For those who were duly licensed, salmon and sea trout netting was an honoured tradition. Generations of fishing families have earned their living this way, and even thrived on their hard toil, but recent years have seen changes. The Tamar estuary no longer supports great runs of profitable bass, and the sudden bonus of a great shoal of mullet is nowadays rare. The waters are almost fished out, apart from the salmon runs, and they too have diminished, thus it was—and still is—important that illegal netsmen be discouraged most vigorously.

In the early part of the season, poachers using multi-monofilament nets were always variously active on any one or more of the entrances to the Rivers Tamar, Lynher and Tavy. It was not easy for us to cover them all, and without good information we would never have been able to record any success in stopping poaching on a scale which, if unchecked, would have ruined salmon fishing in these rivers for ever. Both local poachers and those who came from up-country were highly professional, well equipped and totally ruthless. Neither lot cared about the future of salmon in the West Country. Both were concerned only with short-term profit at whatever cost to future stocks. They were motivated solely by greed and a strong distaste for any form of conventional work. In character, they were far from being the

Long-tailed field mouse

stereotyped, jolly rustic who steals only for his own pot. Some of them were as potentially violent as any bank-robber, and most of them nourished a strong and active hatred for river wardens. They were not, of course, friends to those who had held and paid for licences over many years, so we were not bereft of informants among the latter; indeed, many of our successes derived from their warnings. But our resources were few and widely stretched; we won battles, but the war is even now not ended and the incoming grilse are still at risk from indiscriminate men who take anything and everything without thought for the fishing tomorrow.

OPPOSITE
*A sea trout smolt,
together with bright-yellow
celandine*

Every year as a bailiff I always looked forward to seeing the beginnings of the smolts' peregrinations downstream. What makes them leave their home waters for the distant sea is one of the natural mysteries which man has not yet unravelled. If we could get into their minds, if they have minds, it would not be hard to imagine that they might be feeling a bit tremulous at this stage in their development, like teenagers leaving a secure and comfortable home for university or their first jobs. But smolts have the advantage of migrating in numbers, with a host of like-minded travelling companions, playing team-games together (or perhaps piscine formation dancing?) as they make their adventurous way towards the sea. Lucky walkers on the upper moor may see them indulging in these high jinks, which are described hereabouts as 'dimpling'.

Perhaps these pre-travel rituals are an annual smolt salute to spring, much as madrigals on Magdalen Tower betoken the coming of the Oxford summer. Whatever they are, the sight is not easily forgotten, nor will those who see it ever again fail to distinguish smolts from trout, even in the murkiest of water. Every year, usually in April, the smolts gather in the pools in the higher reaches of our rivers and leap up and down to buss the surface of the water like demented scuba divers. The dance is not part of a feeding pattern, but simply some sort of game they play as they move from pool to pool. Perhaps it is a form of initiation rite, or a final fling and a farewell to childhood before they reach the English Channel. Whatever it is, the sight is intriguing. But even if

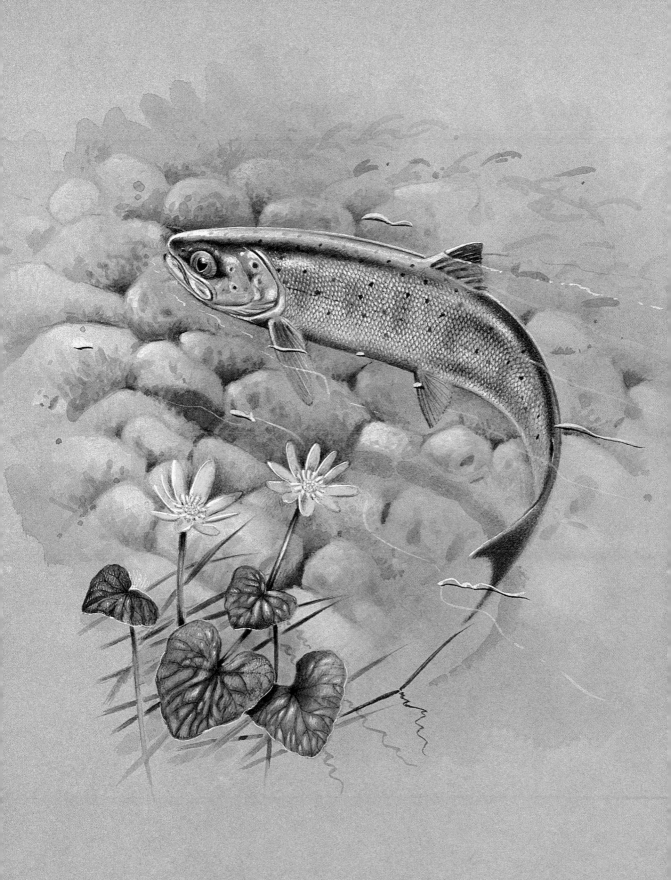

you are privileged to see it, you may still have difficulty trying to decide whether you are watching the progeny of sea trout or salmon. If so, take heart—the salmon smolts are smaller and more immature-looking than the smolts of sea trout; they are also prettier and have blunter heads.

The shoaling of the smolts is an impressive spectacle, and a sign of spring as reliable as the ending of a badger's hibernation, or the coming of the chiff-chaffs. Their migration indicates that the rivers have come alive again; the shiny silvering of their bodies which occurs before their migration, and their progress downstream tells us that all is still well with the river system. So too, in the other direction, do the first returning 'springers', in advance of the main body which will come later in April and early May, fighting upstream against waters swollen by late snow on the hills, but quite certain of the direction they are taking towards the place of their birth.

The smolt migration will go on through April to finish in May. I used to watch them at Lopwell Dam, two or three miles away from the estuary where the Tavy joins the Tamar, and wonder how long their carefree leapings would continue once they reached their oceanic destination. Once there, they would start to grow very quickly indeed, putting on almost seven pounds in a year in the case of salmon. The weight gains of the sea trout are less impressive despite their being larger than salmon smolts when they leave the rivers, but then they will not be travelling so far nor so adventurously. Hugging the shoreline of the Channel coast, they will return to Devon after a year or so weighing not much more than a couple of pounds. There are exceptions to this. Fish that are solitary and experienced and have returned to the river on previous occasions may sometimes grow to between ten and fifteen pounds, but they are rare, and the casual angler is unlikely to meet them.

Keeping an eye on the smolt migration involved more than simply watching their progress downriver. Until effective screens were introduced, preventing smolt from boldly going where even the boldest smolt ought not to go, the annual Tavy smolt rescue was a highlight of the spring season. In its day, because it brought all the bailiffs together close to the town and in sight of a curious

The Lopwell Dam salmon steps are invaluable at migration time for the leaping 'springers'

public, it was a welcome diversion from normal routine; but one year it ended (as diversions often do) in tears. On that fated rescue, I still look back with a mixture of amusement and sorrow that I ever allowed it to loom so large in my working life.

Every year, a large number of smolt would be sucked into the canal which begins in water diverted from the Tavy, near Abbey Bridge in Tavistock, and then flows serenely south west to Morwhellham on the banks of its big sister, the Tamar. Here at its destination the waters are diverted, in a manner guaranteed to please conservationists everywhere, to make electricity.

I approved of the canal, even if I didn't approve of smolts getting into it and becoming at risk of entering the turbines downstream: they were too precious to the future of the Tavy's salmon and sea trout stock to suffer such an ignominious death. So ten of us under the Head Bailiff would gather every year to rescue the strays by stunning them with an electric probe and then putting them back, as quickly as possible, into the main river.

We worked in two teams of five armed with buckets, one moving downstream from the town end and the other working upstream from a point near Morwhellham. A water tanker accompanied the latter team because the part of the canal they covered was too far from the river for the stunned fish to be transferred by bucket. Each team had a portable generator, a man operating the electric probe, a couple of netsmen to pick up the stunned fish and another two bucketmen to carry the fish back to the main river or, at the Morwhellham end, place them in the temporary refuge afforded by the tanker. Since the fish had to go back into water as speedily as possible after their traumatic shock, the 'town end' bucketmen needed to hump their heavy burdens as best they could at a kind of loping and ungainly trot, making them a very peculiar spectacle. The curious mothers and children who watched us at work usually stayed at a safe distance: a group of

Large sea trout

weather-beaten men in waders and oil-skins, carrying things across the children's playground in plastic buckets could not have been a very reassuring sight.

Each team, in the time-honoured tradition of workmen called upon to divide a task between them, thought itself badly done by. The whingers by the playground thought themselves unlucky because they had to carry buckets to the river when the other team could put their stunned fish straight into the water tanker: the whiners at the Morwhellham end cursed their luck at being outside the town. There was always some dispute as to which team did the most work, and whose lot was the most enviable. But it was not an argument into which I entered much, because I had worked on both teams at different times and, more importantly, these smolt were 'mine' and all that concerned me was to get them back into the right water before they died. The Tavy was 'my' river and I didn't want to see it deprived of fish: more than the others, perhaps, I wanted the smolt rescue to be successful.

On this particular day, the 'town end' team worked hard and quickly. We soon arrived at a point where the river was too far away for us to carry the rescued fish there, so I trudged on with two buckets to where I thought the tanker would be stationed below the school. When I arrived, there was no sign of it. I waited—ten, fifteen, then twenty minutes. By this time, the future salmon and sea trout stocks which were lurking uncomfortably in my buckets were looking distinctly gloomy. I decided, much against the grain, that they had better be returned to the canal whence they came. There was nothing else I could do with them, so in they went to face the hazards of the turbines. I pushed on, testily, with my empty buckets, to find out what had happened to the tanker.

There was quite a way to walk before I reached it, to find my opposite numbers blithely taking their ease, although that was not how I mentally described their lack of activity. Mildly, or so I thought (they may have thought otherwise), I registered my disapproval. I really was concerned to get as many smolts back into the river as I could, and the sight of my fellow bailiffs' apparent indifference to this objective riled me more than perhaps was wise. I expostulated. The tanker driver cursed and drove off

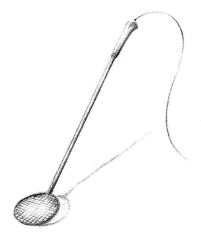

Electric fishing probe

Wood-pigeon standing sentinel

towards the school playing fields while I vainly tried to catch up. Argument, punctuated by many undeleted expletives, and worse, followed. I complained; someone else complained about me: we were both blemished, and the outcome did neither of us much good in the eyes of the Authority.

It was a sad end to what was otherwise a worthwhile day. At the time, the wounds burned deep, and what I thought to be injustice rankled. Even now, I still carry some of the resentments which I then felt. But the recording angel, if he (or she) takes note of such trivia, must have found it all a storm in a relatively small fish bucket. But the incident proves that bailiffs are less imperturbable than they look. And considerably more passionate about their work, and the charges for which they are responsible, than many people may imagine them to be.

Fortunately, there were many other ways of helping smolt than carting them about in buckets. Sometimes, we penned, counted, weighed, measured and micro-tagged them so that scientists could find how they subsequently fared in the shadow of the new Roadford Reservoir—an ambitious project taking up many acres

The song of the returning chiff-chaff is a familiar sound

of land in North Devon and designed to supply water to the increasing population of a rapidly growing Plymouth. Its original siting on Dartmoor had been subject to much opposition. Now, at its new site at Roadford, no one quite knew how it might affect the river system, hence the need for research in which I was glad to take a small part. Other public bodies, I fear, would have been less scrupulous, putting the need for new housing, or new factories, before any possible losses of countryside amenity. Whatever its other deficiencies, at least I was working for an Authority that examined the environmental aspects of its new construction.

Halfway through spring and butterflies begin to appear; otters are occasionally seen playing on certain river banks, diving down slides like errant children; clumps of primroses enliven the woods at Double Waters, and willow-warblers and chiff-chaffs, better portents of the summer to come than cuckoos, begin to sing praises at being back once more in the 'sceptred isle'. I also acknowledge the season and start to fish for brown trout on the high moor. Everything is vibrant. Every bud and flower shouts with new life. Every river, at least when the banks have recovered from the floods and the dead wood and the detritus have been cleared out, looks newly reborn to its pristine state. The number of paintworthy subjects increases with every passing day. The artist in me yearns for more time to paint and the fisherman, more time to fish.

May perhaps is an even better month, when one can see the same river bank at a slightly warmer level of verdancy. Choosing the best time of the West Country year is never easy, but this may be it; the time when even the most cynical begin to believe in a brighter future, and down-to-earth bailiffs wouldn't be surprised if they saw little green men in Grenofen woods, and salmon dancing eightsome reels in the pools below Denham Bridge. In my last year as a bailiff, brimstone butterflies were here in greater profusion than ever, attracted to my cottage garden by the ivy I'd planted round every tree sturdy enough to foster it.

Late spring birds, too, are a delight at this time. I enjoy simply seeing and listening to them, but to know their names is even more rewarding. I can't claim omniscience, but I can recognize most of our commonest visitors, like the willow-warbler and the chiff-chaff. These are rather special birds, so close to being look-alikes that the only way for all but keen ornithologists to tell them apart is by their songs. When I hear their disparate airs, drifting out of the trees along the banks of the lower Tavy, I know that I can safely cast any clouts to which I may still be over-cautiously clinging. Springtime and early summer are still the most hopeful seasons, bringing with them all manner of changes.

Birdwatching is part of my life. Not the long, lying-in-waiting sort, but just the casual concomitant of a daily round that takes me to places where birds are likely to be found. Quite often I'll see a heron, patiently standing on one leg awaiting the false move of a small trout, or a kingfisher perched on a branch on the riverside, ready to belly-flop into a pool for a minnow, both birds which visitors might never see in the whole course of their holiday. So I am lucky; even the routine parts of my work produce rich bonuses of rare natural sights and sounds.

As the days get warmer, the pressure of work increases. Nothing much is going on at this time upriver, but downstream is a different story. The seaward reaches of the rivers are beginning to fill with the comings and goings of salmon, sea trout, smolts and even some kelts, fish which have spawned and reverted to their bright silver migratory colour, to return, exhausted, to the sea. Not everyone can recognize the difference between these and fresh-run fish at first glance, but look at them sideways and you can easily distinguish them. The kelt is thin and flat-bellied and undernourished, lacking the nicely-rounded stomach of the well-fed, sea-wintered fish, and having the frayed and weathered, or even torn and ravaged gill-rakers which indicate the presence of gill-maggots.

Most of my duties at this time were concerned with the rivers' lower reaches. Not all of them were as pleasant as those which took me about the estuary to talk to the legal netsmen and professional fishermen who nowadays face an uncertain future. On those trips I was meant to be gathering intelligence about fish and poachers, but I inevitably also heard many tales of the old days, when fish were plentiful and the bass, always with a ready market, charged into Plymouth Sound in huge quantities. Perhaps these men never made much more than a moderate return for the life they led, despite occasional shoals which brought them a bonus, but at least they were not conscious, as they are now, that they might soon see the foundations of their lives completely eroded. Illegal netting was killing their livelihoods. Poachers with fast boats and huge nets were sweeping up salmon in quantities which almost guaranteed progressive decline in future stocks. It was essential that we stopped them before the salmon disappeared entirely.

The picture they painted to me was a gloomy one, even if the reality was not perhaps quite as gloomy as my friends made out. The new breed of professional poachers was indeed a menace. They were well equipped with faster boats than ours, and they had all the advantages of an attacker who could mount surprise strikes in any of a dozen places. On the face of it, the odds were against us. We could only try to out-think them, guessing, often wrongly, where they might be. And even when we guessed right, they

usually had enough time to dispose of any evidence of their activities, mocking us in our impotence. But over the years since my first estuary patrol, our resources had steadily improved. We had better and faster boats, we had more people coming forward with information, and we began to get the latest night sights, which allowed us, almost literally, to see in the dark. In addition, our patrols along the lower reaches of the rivers were proving quite effective, with magistrates becoming less inclined to deal gently with proven offenders than they had been some years earlier when, after one of my first successful prosecutions, I remember one accused was fined £70, a sum he could earn more than twice over in a single night's work. I still have a copy of the note I wrote expressing my dismay at the unsatisfactory end to a case which had cost much time and personal effort to bring to a successful prosecution.

Young rabbits are a common springtime sight in the West Country

By the mid-1980s, the Bench had become more stern. Magistrates began to recognize that they were dealing with large-scale crime, from which a few organized gangs were making rich pickings, and they began to adjust their sentences accordingly. The flourishing Continental market for stolen salmon remained, but a new Act had made life more difficult for those native hoteliers and others who were accustomed to accepting fish from strangers at the back door, 'no-questions-asked'. Now, the onus of proving the legitimacy of a salmon's origin lay with the receiver. Bland pleas of ignorance were no defence, and it became incumbent upon casual salmon buyers to justify the source of their 'bargain' fish. At least one old outlet for stolen fish was effectively contained.

Bailiffs were always busy in spring, but our working patterns did allow some days for one's own fishing. Long and unsocial hours could be followed by two days off-duty when the rest of the world was sitting at an office desk. On such days, crisp and fine, if one was lucky, I would head for the high moor and tackle the brown trout on the upper reaches of the Tavy or the Walkham. It was a busman's holiday in one sense, since I needed to do more than drive a car to a chosen rendezvous and step out next to my chosen pool. On the upper moor, life was more complicated and difficult than that: I was going to have to walk, and perhaps quite a long way.

I also had to know whether the river, which would be accounted little more than a stream in other parts, was running fast or slow; whether the secret pools were full or emptying. I needed to choose my rod and my flies with care, and no second thoughts, because I could not expect to clamber about the bogs and boulders of the high valleys laden with a selection of Hardy's finest. One rod and a minimum of bags and encumbrances was all I could allow myself, since to achieve anything, I would almost certainly have to move from place to place.

Angling literature is full of joyous accounts of fishing small streams for wild brown trout. For this really is fishing at its least artificial. Up on the moors there are no stocked rainbows, no fishing huts to which to retire when the weather becomes inclement, no pubs less than a few miles' walk away. It is far

OPPOSITE
An Emperor dragonfly at rest on a twig

removed from the civilized and relatively immobile style of fishing one meets on artificial trout lakes and slow chalk streams, where men pursue a laid-back battle of wits with trout who have met humans before. On the moor, a young trout will be as surprised to see you as you will be to see him. Unlike the specimens which fatly cruise the placid waters of the Test or Itchen, showing themselves off with all the confidence of fish that have been chased before, the moor trout is a small, lean, fast-moving package of nervous energy, quite unfamiliar with man's potential inhumanity to fish. But it will also have led a hard, under-privileged life which makes it distrust anything or anyone unfamiliar. Unlike those Stockbridge trout which glide about the stream in the main street to the 'oohs' and 'aahs' of the tourists for whom they perform daily, it won't show off.

Like me, there were plenty of local family men who fished the moorland streams for pleasure, but who also welcomed the cheap protein their fishing provided. For them, used to taking no more than a few brown trout, the occasional salmon was a rich bonus. And such salmon were indeed found a surprisingly long way upstream, in places no outsider would dream of looking for them. Although most were taken legally, further towards the rivers' mouth some were taken illegally, so it was there that I used to do most of my spring enforcement work. When I was not patrolling the estuary, I mostly watched for poachers on the reaches of the Walkham and Tavy rivers just south and west of Tavistock. The job required patience, some fieldcraft and a sixth, seventh and eighth sense of where one's quarry was likely to be operating on the day one chose to stalk them. By patrolling the area, receiving reports of suspicious characters seen loitering near well-known, productive pools and from local gossip—or merely from my own gut feeling—I could make a sound, informed guess that somebody, or more likely some two or three bodies, were poaching at a particular place. I would then arrange with one of my colleagues for us to set up a watch at a time the poachers were most likely to be present, and settle down to wait. Quite often it was a long and unproductive wait, for either the miscreants had spotted our car, or seen us on an earlier patrol, or even been told of our presence by some friend who had had his own brushes with us in the past. But even if we actually saw someone obviously poaching, it was not enough simply to take them without evidence that would stand up in court against a smart lawyer and a defendant to whom truth meant nought. Even habitual poachers are innocent until *proven* guilty.

Sometimes, though rarely, the observation was short and straightforward, and led to a satisfying conviction. Once, for example, we had information that a motor-cycle and scooter were parked close to the Tavy near Tavistock. The motor-cycle, the registration number of which had previously been circulated, was suspected of having been used in earlier poaching incidents, so I took up a position with a colleague where we could watch the nearby river and the two motor-cycles. We waited for about two hours, a long time when you cannot move freely, nor do anything which might attract attention to your presence. It was on vigils like this that I would sometimes make sketches of birds in my notebook (which later led to accusations of breaching the rules) to pass the time; usually, though, I simply listened and watched the wildlife around me.

This time, our observation paid off. Just as we were beginning to get restive, three men emerged from a hedge beside the river carrying a yellow plastic bag. When we approached to question them, they fled, dropping the bag in which we found a salmon, a sea trout, a face mask and a wire snare. After catching all three of them, they admitted they had used the snare to take fish illegally and were subsequently charged.

Not all cases were quite so uncomplicated. Accused people, unless they were caught in possession of fish or snares or similar impedimenta, could dream up a thousand reasons for being on the river which, without evidence to the contrary, were difficult to refute. Most of the river poachers favoured snares, made from an ordinary wire which slips over the salmon's tail when it is resting below an overhang, or a snatch—a three-pronged hook which is positioned beneath the fish then jerked up so that the tines dig into the fish's side. Both of these methods leave irrefutable marks, so no restaurateur in this area can have any excuse for accepting such fish, and anyone carrying either snare or snatch is almost certainly up to anything but good. It was harder to pin down the estuary people, since there is nothing in itself illegal in carrying a net—it was the use to which it was put that counted, and that was always difficult to prove.

The delightful early purple orchid flowers from April to June

The light in a Devon May excites anyone who even pretends to paint, and the countryside provides a mass of subjects which clamour to be painted. Skies are often bright and clear, unmarred by summer haze, and the glorious light comes in like winter sunshine, low and slanting through the trees on the river's edge, creating scenes of incredible beauty. Down from Double Waters, where the Tavy merges with the Walkham, and past the cottage of a lady who has fished here for over forty years, few people ever walk. Yet the river at this point is enchanting, and the river bank is rich in trees and spring flowers. This place, so close to the families picnicking further upstream, has a heron and a family of buzzards circling the high pines on the private bank opposite and fish which rise happily in the knowledge that very few anglers will appear to tempt them.

Working in such a place was like taking a holiday and being paid for so doing. Occasionally, on days off and with permission from an owner, I would get the chance to do my own fishing on these reaches, usually for an early run of small summer salmon, about seven to twelve pounds perhaps, and livelier than the larger springers. I used to fish for them with a tube or a Waddington, or sometimes an Esmond Drury hook lightly dressed with an orange and yellow bucktail, for which different districts had different names. With the addition of a Jungle Cock Eye, for example, Dart fishermen call it a 'Dart Black', notwithstanding its colour, and praise it highly. Using an 11-foot, Hardy Wye rod and a $3^1/_4$-inch Zenith or Hardy Perfect reel—an outfit light enough to carry about all day without pain—I found it worked very well. Wryly, I must add that springtime sees Tavistock schoolboys doing as well as I with nothing more than cheap rods and hunks of cheese.

When the end of May approached and the beginning of summer could be detected in warmer south-westerlies and the increased clamour of birds and insects, I would usually end the month doing more patrols of the estuary, where the illegal netsmen were still

busy. Then, having stored up a few days' leave, and safely banked my salary cheque, I would make a trip to the Kennet, for what the chalk-stream men might claim to be proper fly-fishing. I shan't argue. I enjoy most kinds of fishing and recognize the different skills demanded for each. And no fisherman, not even the most devoted to his own particular speciality, could possibly not enjoy the mayfly season on a Hampshire chalk stream.

A pair of buzzards rising in a thermal

CHAPTER TWO

HIGH SUMMER AND LOW WATER

The wood white butterfly,
seen in the summer

My holiday ends too soon. The great clouds of dancing mayflies disappear as suddenly as they came, and the duffers depart, satisfied with their catches and the ease of their fishing. In truth, the trout between Hungerford and Kintbury have been driven daft by the surfeit of rich feed which appears at this time of the year, and even the clumsiest of tyros could take them. But I enjoyed basking in the sybaritic pleasures of a stay with friend and fellow fisherman David Channing-Williams, and I depart well content from the lush pastures of a Hampshire which is just beginning to burgeon into high summer.

This is gentler country than mine, soft and pastoral, with fatter cattle and villages more prosperous and snug. The tors of Dartmoor seem very stern and wild compared with the meadows bordering the Kennet and Test, where the fish reflect their surroundings, being plumper and (except during the mayfly season, when they act out of character) more sophisticated than the impish creatures of our moorland streams. Even the fishermen look better dressed here than they do in Devon, and they certainly carry more expensive tackle than you are likely to find on the banks of the Walkham.

But I am not over-jealous. Hampshire and Berkshire are the sort of counties from which people travel to Ascot and Glyndebourne, Wimbledon and Palace garden parties; where the English Season, crowded with champagne and strawberry receptions, is still celebrated in all its expensive finery. It seems fitting, somehow, that the fish of these prosperous shires should at least appear to be fairer and fatter than those residing elsewhere. Or is it simply the nature of the pellucid chalk stream to magnify the size and enhance the handsomeness of its home-fed trout? For whatever reason, both chalk-stream fish and chalk-stream countryside reflect an assurance that is hard to match. The fish glide lazily in their transparent depths; the rivers flow slowly, confident that they will reach the sea with no need to rush; the houses sit smugly in green glades, proof against wind and storm, and the anglers all look as though they were painted into the landscape many years ago, and nothing will ever remove them. If I say that I am not over-jealous of this up-country life-style, perhaps I am being slightly less than honest. It is hard not to leave all this assured comfort without feeling a mite discontented with my more spartan lot.

The discontent does not last. Driving back down the A38, having decided to return via the moor rather than Okehampton, I see again the stark hills of the National Park, broodingly beautiful if less domestic than the hills of Wiltshire, and feel once more the pull of home. A few miles west of Ashburton and I am back in my own territory, the place where I live and work and draw my wages. Not all of Devon is soft farmland and cream teas. The people who work these boulder-strewn Dartmoor pastures have to be true sons of sparse soil; hardy, shrewd and thrifty if they are to survive. They often infuriate me, but I admire them. Nothing they have was gained without much toil; everything they own could be wiped out in one vile winter. Barley barons are unknown down here, and most moor farmers are happy if they can avoid an overdraft.

Time, though, to turn my mind to my own job. As I drive, I cast a professional eye over the grass to seek clues as to the state of the rivers, wondering what will greet me when I return to duty. Too much brown and I know that the water will be low, for we depend on immediate rainfall for our angling sustenance. There is no acquifer, no underground reservoir to top up deficiencies in precipitation. What comes down tends to dissipate straight away, rather than be absorbed into caverns underground. Most rain runs

Robin Armstrong

off the sides of the hills almost as quickly as it might do from a sloping roof.

I exaggerate only to make a point. June can be a good month for West Country fishermen, provided there is enough water in the rivers and sea trout and salmon, urged on by those instincts which we may never understand, are able to move through the system towards their breeding grounds. In these conditions, opportunities to catch a worthwhile fish present themselves everywhere. But if the weather is fine and very dry, then rivers like the Tavy and the Walkham, having no acquifer to draw upon, become very low. The fish cannot move and need to 'root up' in midstream pools, waiting for sufficient water in which to swim onwards and upwards. In such pools, salmon are very vulnerable to poachers using snares, usually by night, and we are kept busy watching the places where we (and the poachers) know fish to be.

Night work is difficult. Aimlessly stalking the river banks in the hope of catching a poacher by day is hopeless enough, but by night it is even more futile. We therefore need to know where the fish are, so as to anticipate where and when the poachers might try to work, and get there before they do. If we are not in place before they arrive, we are less likely to catch them.

Traversing woods in the dark is not easy. Exercising fieldcraft by day is one thing, but avoiding twigs and branches and loose stones by night is quite another. Usually, therefore, we have to rely on 'information received', a tip-off telling where so-and-so is likely to be operating on a particular night. We can then take up a vantage point above the ear-marked pool; watch the villains as they arrive and (if all goes according to plan) pick them up, with all the evidence of lamps and snares, in the middle of their nefarious business. More commonly, we spend our hours watching the stars, desperate (before I gave up smoking) for a cigarette and wishing we were safely back in bed. Except in the rarest of cases, catching poachers red-handed is a hit-and-miss business which ends more often in frustration than fulfilment; in failure rather than success. Like a policeman, a bailiff on enforcement work mostly endures several hours of boredom for every minute of excitement.

If, as a bailiff, I sometimes wearied of being out at night, there

OPPOSITE
A pair of common blue butterflies

Salmon smolt 'dimpling' the water's surface

were fishermen who did not. These were the 'moonlighters'—licensed sportsmen and earnest seekers after sea trout who came to the river in the months of June and July and fished mainly after dark, or 'after dipsy' as we say here. I have practised such fishing and enjoyed it, but I was not a devotee, and I can understand those anglers who find it a strange, and somewhat cold, addiction. However balmy the English summer day, the night which follows will be chilly, and not everyone can endure it with equanimity. But the night-fishers do, taking their places on the midnight bank much as they would during the day.

There are two sorts of night anglers—those who fish right through until dawn and those who fish for an hour or two after sunset, returning home in time to get some sleep before the start of a new working day. The former have more stamina, or sometimes, as one Devonian cynic expressed it to me, less interest in their wives: the latter have more sense. I take a neutral view, but have to advise those who have never night-fished, that it can be a very daunting experience. Newcomers to it will not always find the sky star-filled, nor the water easily judged. Night sounds, too, are distracting, if not sometimes frightening. We all know that there is nothing in England, neither animal nor once-human, to harm us. Nonetheless, the scream of a night-time vixen calling for its mate; the sudden screech of a barn owl, or even the small rustling of a scurrying vole can acquire sinister undertones. When you are alone by a cold river, at the bottom of a valley edged by black woods, the secret sounds of nature's night-life can some-times send prickles through the most slicked-back hair.

Once you become familiar with the night sounds, you can begin to concentrate on your main business, which is to catch fish. Those who are experienced will have learned to move quietly in the dark and to become at one with their surroundings. They will recognize the thwack and plop of sea trout leaping and crashing about in the pools, and the squeaks of small mammals going about their nocturnal duties, and even perhaps distinguish the grunt of a badger as he plods along his habitual track. I have had much pleasure from night fishing in the past, some of which has lain in recognizing these sounds and feeling part of them, seeing myself as one more night creature pitting his elemental wits and skills against nature with no help from anyone else. Now, with the passing of the years, these pleasures have diminished. I can look back on night fishing with affection, but I actually prefer to do my sea trouting by day, when I can see and not just hear what is going on around me.

Like it or not, however, duty often brings me to the night-time river, since where legitimate anglers are finding fish, you can be sure that poachers will be doing the same. And since cloudless summer nights are rarely so black that you cannot see the shape of things and people against the background of the sky, we do have some chance of spotting the villains, if only as shadowy figures fleeing at our approach—too often, I fear, to get away, unless we stumble on their cars or motorbikes first, and find the implements which can be used as evidence of their guilt.

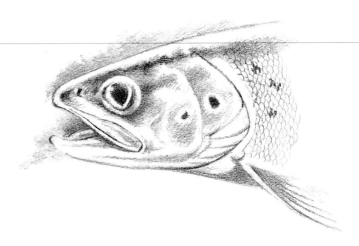

Detail of the head of a smolt sea trout

Ｈigh summer in Devon is the time when everything animal and vegetable is vibrant with life, and even slow humans acquire new zest. We expand in the sunshine and work better when we are not coughing and sniffling, or obsessed with keeping warm. We become leaner and keener to get to grips with work; more aware and sensitive to what is going on around us. Once, waking very early on a July morning, I knew I had to get up and out into the fresh dawn sunshine which was trying to pierce the wisps of Walkham Valley mist. I was restless, eager to start the day well. Even at that hour, I knew that later on, it was going to be fine and hot. Nothing much stirred. The birds had ceased, temporarily, their pre-dawn chorus and the insects were still asleep. The grass near the river was an unblemished green carpet, wet with dew: no one could have walked there without leaving tracks.

At this time of the day, all one's senses are alert, and the presence of other humans soon becomes evident. If they smoke, then the scent of tobacco will hang in the still air for many minutes; if they cough, the sound will carry for dozens of yards; if they move, then surely they will rouse a wrathful jay. Stand perfectly still; watch and listen, and unless the intruder on your patch is as immobile as you are, then you cannot fail to detect him.

That morning, I knew that poachers had been about. But I was too late for them. They had already gone. They had left no tracks

in the dew, nor broken any twigs in negotiating the hedge. They had been too careful to smoke and too practised to make a noise, for they were no doubt as experienced as I was. What had become second nature to me was also second nature to them: poachers who work the rivers, rather than simply attacking the estuaries with crude nets, are as skilled in fieldcraft as any bailiff.

If there were no visible signs or smells of my adversaries, how did I know they had been there? Perhaps I had simply imagined them; perhaps I was simply becoming over-sensitive to the point of idiocy, pretending to higher powers I simply did not have. I think not. Ask any bailiff and he will tell you that he always knows when someone has been on his immediate patch. He won't be able to say how he knows, and if he tries to explain, he is unlikely to be anything but incoherent. He simply knows, and he will tell you so, very flatly, and with complete assurance.

Early on, when I was first learning my country trade, I had admired an old Dartmoor farmer who had crept close enough to two poachers to photograph them in their larceny.

'How did you manage it?' I asked.

'Well, boy!' he replied, 'I don't step on no twigs, see!'

I knew what he meant. Not stepping on twigs; moving smoothly and quietly; staying still when necessary and being able

Two salmon fry

to exercise the patience of a cat which knows of the mouse beneath the dresser, are essential qualities in a bailiff. Without them, he cannot ever hope to do a good job.

The basic virtues I would seek in any applicant for my job are much the same as those possessed by a successful angler. Both need knowledge and the perseverance to exercise it constructively. Both need to accept set-backs with equanimity and to learn from their mistakes, and both need to recognize that their respective mysteries are ones in which the learning process never ends. If I had stayed a bailiff for the rest of my life, my knowledge of rivers and fish (not to mention the quirks of fishermen) would still not be complete, despite all that I learned from the different jobs which were given to us.

Stock surveying, for example, was one regular summer research task. This involved stop-netting a section of a river so that nothing could escape from either end of the sample reach; 'fishing' it three times with electro-fishing equipment, and counting, weighing and measuring the fish each time. It was a tedious job, but worth doing. Experience of a 1983 survey into the distribution of fish in the River Tavy and its tributaries, made under the supervision of Hugh Sambrook, one of the Water Authority's scientists, had more than convinced me of the value of objective research. By carefully counting and measuring fish by type, analysing the chemistry of the water at various points, and assessing the effects of both water abstraction and discharges from local sewage treatment works, we were able to draw up a unique picture of what was happening in the river, and why. It was an instructive piece of work.

Throughout my life, I had read fishing books, some of which went into much technical detail, but I had never before seen a report which examined fish life so methodically and in such measured statistics. This was my first real sight of the scientists' contribution to angling's welfare, and one which I could very much support. Puffing strong pipes in the old pubs, and shaking their sage heads pessimistically as they talked, local countrymen could proffer a dozen explanations for the decline in salmon runs, or the fall in trout numbers on certain streams. But they could never match science in knowing which of the explanations was most important, and what action would most efficiently improve things. Working on surveys and in the hatcheries watching scientists pursuing their careful ways, turned me into a confirmed believer in the value of pure research—provided it was backed up by the experience of fishermen who actually knew the water. It may seem self-evident to say that if our rivers are to be preserved, practical men must respect and co-operate with their backroom cousins, but even today, I still occasionally meet those who have no time for theoretical investigation. 'If there is money to spend, then spend it on improvements, not surveys and backroom studies', they say, refusing to recognize that we first need to know which improvements are likely to produce the best returns.

OPPOSITE

The yellow flag iris is often seen alongside rivers or on marshy ground in summer

The month of July is a less romantic one than June, and so (apart from the Glorious Twelfth) is August, perhaps because finding loving rhymes for them is difficult. But in this part of the world they are good months for fishing, provided (as I wrote earlier) that the water levels are not too low. When they are, we get 'backers'—newly arriving fish that come in with the tide only to find that because of the fish already waiting, they cannot move on . They then 'back off' into the estuary on the ebb, to wait there until they can get upriver, meanwhile providing rich pickings for legal and illegal netsmen alike.

If there were enough water, the river would, in theory, be full of moving fish, and I should be working upriver to protect them. This year, we have a dry spell and I need to spend my time downstream on the estuaries, trying to stop the potential decimation of fish that are the foundation of our future stocks. To find out about which gangs are operating, I talk, tactfully, to the legal netsmen who have much to lose from poachers, and as little love for them as we have. Even so, few will inform outright on those who take fish without the licences which the legitimate men must pay for. The most they will do is to drop hints and pointers about what is going on unlawfully and where, leaving us to read between the oblique lines of their cautious gossip. It would be nice to have more concrete intelligence, but what we do get is still useful: without it, our job would be impossible.

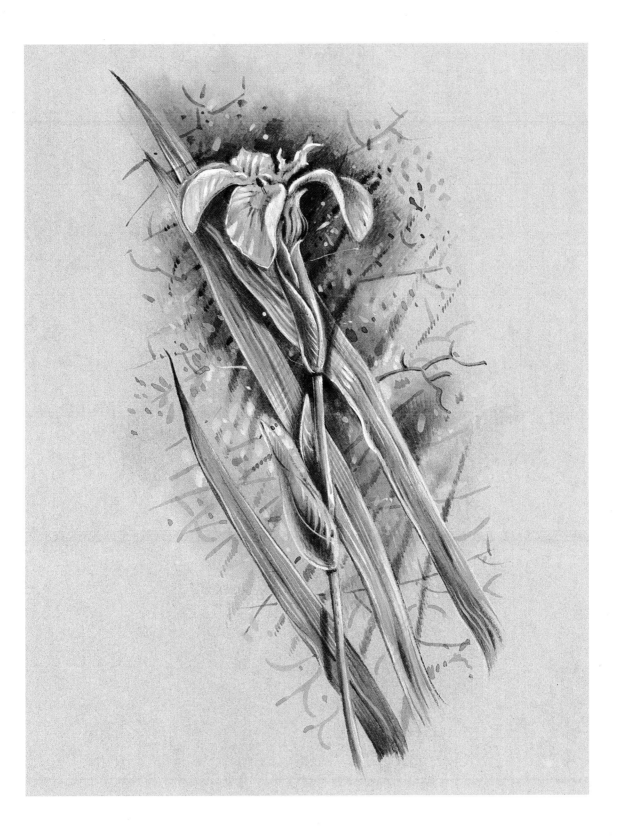

Most of the legal netsmen have been bred to the work. (I suppose the same applies to many poachers.) Their licences have been passed on from father to son for generations and those who hold them know every inch of the estuary's depth and shallows. But their numbers are declining, since there are simply not the stocks to sustain as many as once worked at the business full-time. Alan Jewett, who works on the Tamar, has been netting all his life. He never misses a tide, and nothing happens on the estuary without his knowing it. If his season is poor, then so is that of everyone else. His work rate is prodigious and his strength, if not for the same reason as that of Sir Galahad, is as the strength of ten.

From the viewpoint of tourists who only see him in the height of summer when the chilly north-easters are not gusting across the cold water, his life-style has much to commend it. Rising each day with the sound of the curlew to work a tide, seine-netting in the traditional manner with a two-man team and working together fast and efficently, without need for speech, he spends five, very full days a week living on his houseboat on the river. The two free days are written into his licence to give the fish a reprieve, and a sporting chance to run the river. Even so, taking his preparations into account, he hardly stops work from March until the season ends in August, which is perhaps enough summer work for anyone, and more than enough long days in cramped conditions away from his family.

While he is working, Alan lives with his junior partner, Peter Rainer, who keeps a daily record of everything touching on the life of the river—sightings of birds and mammals, catches, the types of fish found on different days—everything is carefully recorded in a manner that would do credit to the most rigorous of academics.

The days of the big 'net-pulls' of salmon are over. Pictures showing the hauls made by Alan's father tell a story that is unlikely to be repeated. The short-sightedness of professional fishermen, even those who work far away in the Atlantic, has ensured that the catches displayed in them will never be made again. Meanwhile, Alan and his like, fewer in number than they once were, fly the flag of a life-style whose days are numbered. Every so often they have the excitement of a fish which leaps, a 'shearer', to break their routine. Every so often, the sight of mullet dimpling in the estuary

makes them rush out to try for these fish—up to fifteen or twenty
stones in a net-pull and they will have made a tidy profit. But these
shoals, like the once lucrative incursions of summer bass, are in
sad decline. Past overfishing and the careless taking of under-
sized fish have led to present dearth. Short of a miracle, I doubt if
we will ever again see stocks at their old levels.

Alan and his fellows concentrate mainly on netting salmon,
keenly aware that anglers would like their activities to be severely
curbed. I can sympathize with this view. On the other hand, I
think that in the South West at least, although not necessarily
elsewhere, a small amount of strictly controlled netting will do no
harm to salmon's future. It would be sad if honest netsmen
working in time-honoured fashion were to disappear, just because
we cannot catch all the poachers who do the real damage by taking
everything piscine which swims, regardless of its provenance or
its size. If we could only eliminate the poachers, a reduced number
of licensed men could still be permitted to ply their ancient trade.

At one time, of course, the legal seine-netters themselves acted
short-sightedly. In the old days, when commercial fishing in

A pair of ducklings

Britain was a major industry, and few foresaw the decline to come, conservation was hardly an issue. Even until relatively recently, licensed seine-netters were allowed to set fixed nets, tied to the shore at one end and to a buoy at the other. Remorseless and indiscriminate, these nets took in almost everything. Now, a bye-law decrees they must be fixed three metres below sea-level, which gives room for the surface-swimming salmon and sea trout to pass safely into their home rivers.

Dartmoor National Park, which nurtures most of the rivers on which I worked, covers a lot of rugged ground—some 365 square miles of almost empty hills, valleys and moorland. Apart from a few settlements on the peripheries, the high moor is alive to little other than the plaintive moaning of errant lambs, looking for their mothers, and the occasional sound of gunfire from the Army's Okehampton ranges. It is not vast, and the rivers for which we are responsible, such as the Tavy and the Walkham, are less than Amazonian in length, being about 20 miles and 12 miles long, respectively. But distances on the ground are longer than they look on an office map—walking and inspecting all our cherished streams still takes some effort, and rather more time than we can afford with our limited resources.

We therefore enlist all the aid we can, co-operating closely with the National Park wardens, who in their turn co-operate with us by acting as honorary bailiffs, checking fishing licences and keeping watch on suspicious movements; serving as extra eyes and ears and supplying us with the additional bits of intelligence that may make all the difference between success and failure to secure convictions. Even those snippets of gossip which could never be used as the basis of a prosecution are useful in pointing us towards which particular 'firms' are operating in the area. In the summer of 1988, however, our concern was less with poaching than with the old Water Authority shooting itself in the foot by initially declining to say that an outside contractor, finding no one at a water purification plant, had mistakenly tipped some twenty tons of aluminium sulphate into the water supply at Camelford. Although there were reported cases of severe sickness among a large number of people at the time, senior management stayed silent about the matter for several weeks before admitting that a mistake had been made.

The tanker-driver's action was the kind of error that ought never to have happened and would not have happened if the procedures governing the addition of chemical purifiers had not been flouted. But they were, and the Authority knew that things had gone badly wrong. Nonetheless, they refused to acknowledge this wrong for several weeks, while the public were given assurances that turned out to be questionable. The subsequent loss of confidence in the Authority was all the greater for its refusal to admit what had really happened.

Although we were as much in the dark as local residents over what had happened, we knew something was wrong from the reports of dead fish in local rivers. It was some time before the public or anyone else was told the truth about what happened, and

Dartmoor pony

Robin Armstrong '86

the full story is not known to this day. Secrecy and obsession with appearances were, I suppose, the old Authority's worst faults. The job it did was not badly done, but it would have been done better if it had explained more openly to its junior staff and customers exactly what it was about.

The old Authority has now gone and new management is now in place with the National Rivers Authority (NRA) to watch over it. A radical examination of working practices, safety procedures and the like has no doubt been made after the prosecution of the old Authority over the Camelford affair, in keeping with our national genius for closing stable doors after horses have bolted. But better this than nothing, and to be fair, I think (although it is too early to reach a considered judgement) that the new division of responsibilities between private companies supplying the water, and the NRA acting as policeman to our rivers, may work well. Much will depend, however, on the NRA making vigorous use of the powers which have been given to it.

Meanwhile, provided slurry hasn't killed them, mid- to late-summer sees our rivers fill with harvest peal, small sea trout of anything between $1^1/_2$ to 2 pounds. Entering the system, they crowd up in the lower pools and defy us to catch them, and in hot, daytime dry spells they are difficult to take. But provided you are not restricted to 'fly only', you can usually succeed using the pedestrian lure of bread and cheese paste. Find the peal, keep well back on the bank and stay concealed, then cast so as to let your bait float freely through the shoal. Sea trout will always pester small particles moving through the water, not necessarily intending to feed on them, and with any luck, they will pursue your cheese and bread until you can strike—in my case using an 11-foot Mark IV Avon rod with a small fixed-spool reel and a $1^1/_2$ lb line.

Assuming you manage to strike at the right time, you will surely find yourself into a lively sea trout. But your troubles have only just begun. If the shoal vibrates and moves sideways, you will have to guide your fish away from the rest, preferably upstream, all the while making fullest use of your long rod to remain unseen, for once the shoal spots you, your fishing will be over. The purists, of course, will deplore this method, whispering behind their hands that only the unskilled proletarians of fishing would use cheese

OPPOSITE
Young tawny owl

and paste instead of the more aesthetic fly. But if your holiday is short, and your fishing days are limited, and you happen upon a crowd of fish waiting to be taken, then why not be prepared to take them? I think that we who live near trout streams sometimes forget that the bulk of British human kind must drag out their days in cities, far from bubbling brooks and quiet woods. When they do manage to escape to the country for a few hours, they deserve to strike a country trout.

If they are very lucky, they may also meet with one of August's fickle salmon. Fickle, because if the rainfall has been uncertain, alternating between famine and flood, the fish will not be acting in easily predictable ways. Some of them, in a dry spell, will have been forced to lie up in tiny pools which no novice angler would ever think to examine. Others will have gambled on the extra flow which comes with the rain, and chanced their luck at getting through to their next safe pool before the river falls once more. Salmon can survive in less water than we think. As I walk the summer streams, greatly subdued from the tempestuous levels of spring, I marvel that big fish should want to pursue the obstacle course of boulders, rills and persistent shallows that make for such hard going at times of low water, simply in order to travel so far upstream to spawn. But there is method in their travelling madness. Upstream is cleaner water, and gravel and less disturbance. Any salmon foolish enough to lay its eggs nearer the river mouth would lose them all. Further upstream (and I shall not say exactly where, lest the redds be disturbed, or destroyed, by the curious), they have a sporting chance of survival.

They have a sporting chance, too, of not having to wait too long upon a change in the river level. In this part of the world, even when we have very dry summers, there is usually occasional rain somewhere in the rivers' catchment areas. Thus I read from my notebook that on one July day, 'the river (it was the Tavy) is losing height very rapidly'; on the next, and this would not be untypical, I noted that 'the river is rapidly recovering'. If I had not been so concerned when I made the first entry, I might have remembered that the rivers here are always changing, and that salmon are more than adept at seizing their opportunities and running when they can. Unless the weather is very exceptional

OPPOSITE
A shoal of sea trout

Robin Armstrong '88

Young swallow

indeed, as it was in 1976 when we faced week after rainless week of constant sunshine, the chances of migratory fish being unable to reach home-base are fairly slim.

My summer diary records a full life. We were required to keep track of our hours in some detail, and the June, July and August entries read like the diary of a hyperactive Dervish. I was forever chasing from one place to another, working on the estuary one night, up-river the next, and sometimes on both during the same twenty-four hours. Some patrols were routine, others were made in response to tip-offs which proved groundless. All were different, but at the same time part of a wider plan.

Some entries are laconic. 'Saw several big browns not looking happy', is one memory of a trip to Endsleigh, where we had a hatchery. Why they were not happy, I cannot now say. Nor can I remember what, if anything, I did to cheer them up. Trout are not susceptible to the same affectionate treatment as dogs, and those which are 'not looking happy' (were they scowling, I wonder, or simply swimming in an idle manner?) cannot be persuaded to frolic by the offer of a bone. I expect I simply left them to their misery, muttering that they deserved to be caught.

Shortly following this, there was another entry of similar brevity. 'Mr X says Grenofen Pool is going to be done tonight', reads the graphic, if not very elegant report for one cold July day. The call had come at 7.30 in the evening, from a usually reliable informant, so I deliberately swapped duty in order to make use of his confident tip. After some telephoning, I arranged to pick up one colleague at Peter Tavy and another at Gunnislake, several miles away over the Tamar, and then drove back to Grenofen. By the time we arrived at our observation point, it was eleven o'clock, and dark. It was a cold vigil. No one turned up; no one fished; no one disturbed the uncomfortable passing of some three fruitless hours. Eventually,we gave up; uncoiled our rigid limbs, and went back to Gunnislake. The rest of the night was an anti-climax. I drove to Brentor, looked again at Grenofen Pool, dropped off my colleagues where I had picked them up and went home to bed just after dawn.

Nights such as that were not uncommon. Sometimes we fixed up a 'glo-worm' to assist our observations, but it rarely did. It was (I think, although I am not certain) our own 'in-house' invention; a hollow tube with a small light which could only be seen from the angle at which it was directed, namely our observation post. The light came on when a trip, which we usually set near an entrance gate, or a convenient path to the river, was broken. It was one of those good ideas which never quite worked. Far too often, the trip—which had to be made from something that would break without the intruder feeling it—would be triggered by nocturnal animals, or the wind, raising hopes only to dash them. In short, the 'glo-worm' produced far too many false alarms, proving that there are very few short cuts to the successful catching of night-time villains.

A brownie   Night patrols were not always unpleasant, even when they were unproductive. England by day is crowded, noisy and unmysterious. By night, the traffic din is diminished and the trees, especially under a harvest moon, take on fantastic shapes. The quiet and the absence of people bring me to think of an earlier, less urban time, when country-folk believed in witches and hobgoblins and more things in heaven and earth than even the most vivid of tabloid newspapers can imagine. In those days, West Country rivers would have known salmon and sea trout runs far heavier than we ever see, even in the best of years. Old hands can remember when the Tamar estuary was alive with bass, and the rivers, unspoilt by slurry and sewage discharge, were full to overflowing with healthy trout. How much richer they must have been when Plymouth was little more than the tiny harbour of Sutton, and the population the tiniest fraction of what it is now.

Guides to Devon written in the 1960s may contrast the catches of those days unfavourably with those of the past, but I suspect, without access to any accurate records, that fishermen now would find those 1960s numbers more than generous by today's standards. One writer, D. St Leger-Gordon, in *Portrait of Devon* (first published by Robert Hale in 1963), claimed to have seen a shed below Cotehele, half the size of 'an old fashioned railway carriage and piled half-full with great glistening salmon, representing that morning's catch'.

How many other mornings, I wondered, produced the same? The fish had been netted (legally, I assume), and presumably, in those carefree days, with little or no thought for the tomorrow which we have now inherited. The riches then must have seemed limitless, the forebodings of a few percipient writers nothing more than crazy fancies. The same writer also describes the numbers of salmon taken by netting and rod on the Teign, perhaps 1000 and 150 respectively in an average season. If these were typical catches of the time, then perhaps it is not surprising that salmon are now fewer than they were. Clearly, not all our troubles can be ascribed to pollution—some of the blame must be shared by those greedy and vainglorious netsmen and rodmen who denuded the present by taking too much in the past.

Damselfly at rest

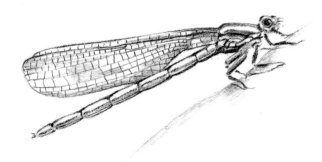

Occasionally working on the Water Authority's reservoirs, I have tried still-water fishing for stocked rainbows. It is a soothing pastime compared with walking the streams of the upper moor. Whether one fishes from the bankside or from one of the Authority's boats, it brings on a great sense of peace and tranquillity. A river is always alive, its mood ever changing, moving and chuckling over stones in constantly shifting patterns. It never sleeps. Still waters are quite different. Even if they do run deep, most lakes lack the character of a brisk river, and I find them less interesting, even if they are more soothing. But fishing is fishing, and I like occasionally to sample what the Water Authority is now vigorously promoting. I have never subscribed to the iconoclastic view that dry-fly fishing on a top trout stream is the one and only kind of fishing. My tastes are more eclectic. I will try anything and, usually, enjoy it.

But I confess that fishing from a boat presents some problems and inconveniences. This way (especially if one has inside information from a friendly keeper) one reaches more fish, but at some cost. No one has yet invented idiot-proof rowlocks, and I usually find myself sprawling among rod and tackle at least once as I make my way to my chosen fishing spot. Even when I reach, panting, where I want to be, I usually spend many anxious

OPPOSITE
A nightingale in full song—a glorious sound

Sea trout chasing a fly, and about to be caught

Grey squirrel

interludes, when retying a fly, trying to stop my unbalanced self and all my gear from falling into the water.

On the whole, therefore, I prefer to sit on the bank, much as I did during my early days as a coarse fisherman. Here I can contemplate nature with an unhurried eye, secure in the knowledge that unless I am very stupid indeed, I am not going to drown, or even get wet. Most of our lakes have some bankside that is reasonably steep, without the long slope which means one may need to wade, so I don't have to contemplate casting huge distances. I therefore usually fish a wet fly with 10-foot rod, a light line and the minimum of effort. If I end up with my quota of rainbows, well and good, I may well throw them back anyway. If I end the day with nothing, I shall not be disappointed, because—so far—our lakes are uncrowded and I can enjoy a day spent beside them whether I catch fish or not.

Mostly, of course, our customers do want to catch fish. Unlike me, they are visitors from afar, on holiday perhaps, with few other opportunities to sample the delights of deepest Devon. During the season, therefore, I usually spend a day or two every month checking the Authority's boats; seeing that the kiosks have not been vandalized and generally keeping an eye on waters whose amenity value is still far from fully realized. As river fishing becomes harder to find, and more expensive, I suspect that lake fishing will boom. Several successful private lake fisheries already provide sport in idyllic surroundings; gourmet restaurants filled with like-minded fellow anglers, and plenty of fat trout for relatively easy taking. In these places, the bailiffs of the future will perhaps become entertainment officers, recruited for their charm and easy manners as much as for their knowledge of fish and fishing.

Until then, we earthier specimens of river wardens must carry on with our humdrum duties. Some day, maybe, if the feat has not already been achieved, artificial trout will be born at will, at the time of year most convenient to lake owners, and bailiffs will then work from nine-to-five like everyone else. Meanwhile, our year follows its ancient cycle. The days shorten; autumn approaches, and a new round of tasks present themselves for my attention. First, though, after some months of often broken sleep, a well-earned holiday.

CHAPTER THREE

POACHER'S MOON

A common tern hovers above the estuary

After a year working on rivers and estuaries with fish and fishermen, it may seem strange that I should come on leave to a place which offers fishing as one of its main attractions. I can only plead that Scotland is different, and that September on the Mull of Kintyre is as good a time and a place to spend a busman's holiday as anywhere I know. The main body of the tourist army has retreated back to Surbiton or Spokane, leaving only the discerning few to an uncrowded Caledonian autumn, full of wonderful colour and seasonal whisky. I come here not just to fish, but to see the wildlife and enjoy the scenery and simply to relax.

Mull of Kintyre fishing, in rivers, lochs and off the coast, is just about perfect. Within a few miles, you can practise every angling art you have ever learnt. As to the small towns, if they attracted fewer tourists, the amenities they offer might be less good; if they attracted many more, then their charm would be lost. The present balance between keeping the area unspoilt and meeting the needs of the local people is, it seems to me, just about right.

For those who enjoy occasional solitude, as I do, there are still many parts of the Mull where you can fish in the sort of splendid isolation which is hard to find outside the Highlands. A mile or two inland, and you will soon have nothing for company but the curlew of the surrounding moors, and, less obviously, the brown trout which dart about in most of the moorland streams. As in

West Devon, all you need for fishing is a light rod and simple tackle, plus a haversack for your lunch and a small flask to keep out the chill, or save you from the sun.

You could, of course, eschew the lure of the uplands and make your way along the Atlantic coast, to watch the breakers thumping ashore in clouds of fine spray. I did this, transfixed by the latent power of the ocean as it unceasingly surges and recedes against the barrier of cliffs. The possibility that someday these same waters will be augmented by a melting ice-cap, to pour down and engulf us all in one gigantic flood is now aired daily. Sensible men finding themselves on the Mull will therefore hasten while they may to hire the right gear to do some sea-angling before the apocalypse. It's an exhilarating pastime, especially from the rocks, where the ever-present danger that a rogue wave may sweep you away into eternity adds spice to the most pedestrian of holidays.

I survive this hazard, partially because I spend more time walking along the coast than I do fishing for cod and mackerel, content to take in the scenery and watch the wheelings and unscrupulous dealings of a wider variety of sea-birds than I see in Devon. Birds' inhumanity to other birds runs just as deeply as that of man: where food and the feeding of children are concerned, no

A trawler fishing off the coast

bird puts itself second, except when superior force compels it to do so.

But holidays end and duty awaits. Robin Armstrong ceases to imagine himself a Scottish laird of independent means, with an inclination to fishing and painting, and reverts to his working bailiff self. Autumn is not over, and back in West Devon there is much to do on river and estuary. As we discuss plans to cover our extensive bailiwick against late-season poachers, I recall one September capture, some three or four years ago when I was not on holiday, and 'a fair cop' had an unexpected outcome.

It was after a spate, and there were a lot of good, fresh salmon in the upper reaches of one of my rivers. And someone, according to our intelligence, was milking them in large numbers. We knew, almost with certainty, who it was likely to be. 'Gaffer' Davy (though this was not his real name) was an experienced poacher whose nefarious fishing career went back over twenty years. He was both skilled and careful, and despite all our efforts, he had rarely been caught.

We had been told what he was doing, and we were impressed. Clad in a wet suit, he was completely immersing himself in the deeper of the river pools, then searching for salmon under the rocky underhangs and among the tree roots by the light of a small torch. It was an adventurous technique, which allowed him to operate in conditions when other poachers could not.

I knew 'Gaffer', and how guileful he was. Containing him would not be easy, and I had especially asked for Ron, our ex-SAS sergeant, to help me in staking-out the pool where we thought he might be working. Our first vigil produced no sighting, but this was not an unusual set-back, and we determined to continue to seek him out. 'Gaffer' was no fool, and as a rogue, he was more likeable and less violent than most. He never seemed to work, except at poaching, although he was clearly capable of mastering several skills. And he was a born countryman, sensitive not only to the near presence of another human, but also alert to the reactions of the surrounding wildlife which might betray that presence. To catch him salmon-handed, as it were, we would have to work with some care.

The first thing was to leave our cars well away from the area of

the pool we expected him to rob, for any sight of them—even within a mile or so of the river—would cause him to abandon his plans. We would also have to approach our target along the hedgerows, rather than across fields where we might be seen. And having reached our projected observation posts, we would have to choose and camouflage our hides as skilfully as any big-game hunter.

In these matters, Ron was my mentor. Arriving at the suspected pool at 2 pm, well in advance of the time we expected 'Gaffer', we set to work with knives, binder twine—not the bright blue plastic sort, but stuff well weathered in mud and dung—and some bits of Army camouflage material. I settled in a small ditch by a hedgerow, with Ron beside a gate by which 'Gaffer' might reach the pool, some fifteen yards away.

For September, it was a hot day. In the hide, it was warm and uncomfortable. I was glad I'd brought refreshment in the shape of a bottle of Lucozade, my stand-by drink on such occasions. I lay quietly, in touch only by radio with the unseen Ron, to whom I confided my concern about a huge black cloud over Meldon, on the high moor to the north east. This, I suspected, might betoken the onset of a thunderstorm, resulting in a flash flood which would raise the water level dramatically in a matter of minutes. If that happened, then 'Gaffer' would not come.

I peered out. From where I lay, I could just see the edge of the pool. Sure enough, the water was beginning to rise and colour-up. I hoped that 'Gaffer' had not noticed the cloud, otherwise he was likely to turn back home. Suddenly, I spotted him. In a one-piece wet suit, and carrying a khaki haversack, he crossed a couple of fields and came within two feet of Ron without seeing him.

At this point, I thought we might go for an arrest, since the haversack clearly didn't contain library books. Almost certainly, we would find poaching equipment in it. But we decided to bide our time.

'Gaffer', true to his reputation, was cautious. A wood-pigeon, flying out of a nearby tree, kept him motionless for at least three or four minutes, as though he were trying to sense an alien presence by sheer will-power. Twice he looked straight in my direction, and twice, under his keen stare, I was tempted to move. But I stayed frozen in the hide, knowing that so long as I remained still, he would not see me. Whether or not he had noticed the state of the water, I couldn't tell. If he had, it cannot have bothered him, because he then began to rummage in the haversack for his equipment. First he drew out a small dark torch, followed by a curious implement which I had never seen before; a kind of gaff hook on the end of a long piece of string, obviously (after I thought about it) intended for salmon jammed tight in the rocky underhangs. To get a snare round fish in these circumstances is difficult—I guessed this was his alternative method of moving them.

'Gaffer' looked doubtfully at the river, pondering whether the water was too murky for his purpose. It was touch and go whether he would carry on or not. I knew there were fish in the pool, and so, presumably, did he, and this must have tempted him. Grasping his strange gaff hook, and his torch, he plunged into the river.

Gaff hook

Although he didn't stay in the water very long, we were ready for him when he came out. It was, it seemed to us, 'a fair cop'. Our evidence, we thought, would stand up in any court. We cautioned him; told him what we had seen; charged him with attempting to take salmon, and left him still wondering how we had managed to get so close without his seeing us. Altogether, we were well content with our afternoon's work.

It takes time for cases to reach trial. In the months that followed, I forgot about our small success, although every so often I felt a slight unease that 'Gaffer' might find some way of wriggling out of his well-deserved misfortune. When we finally got to court, however, Ron and I felt that this time, surely, 'Gaffer' would get his just deserts. The case, we decided, was open and shut.

Just then, 'Gaffer' himself turned up. 'What are you pleading this time, "Gaffer"?' I chaffed him. 'Insanity?'

'Not guilty,' he said defiantly.

'Not guilty?' I repeated. 'Surely you're joking! We got you almost red-handed. What can you say to that?'

'Just you wait and see, boy,' he said. 'Just you wait and see!'

I wasn't in court when 'Gaffer' gave his evidence, but I shall never forget giving mine. Well scrubbed and brushed, and properly be-suited, I told my story simply and convincingly, or so I thought, knowing that right was clearly on my side. But I had not reckoned on 'Gaffer'.

'My client,' said his solicitor, with all the languid aplomb which only an English legal training can give, 'had simply been pursuing his life-long hobby of surfing. In the course of this innocent venture, he had unfortunately lost his treasured St Christopher medal. He had then gone home, collected the gaff hook which you see in evidence, and returned to the river to try, using this ingenious device, to retrieve it.'

Tavistock Court House

The magistrates looked puzzled. The Clerk of the Court, who had heard everything and more before, gave an audible and long-suffering sigh. The public gallery suppressed mild titters. Everyone present knew that surfing is what you do in the sea off north Cornwall. And that in the Tavy, rock-strewn and full of hazards, it is hard enough to find pools in which to swim, much less undertake any other form of water sport. Had 'Gaffer' mentioned water-skiing, his story would have been no more incredible.

And what about the unusual gaff hook? 'Ah, yes!' continued our West Country Rumbold, 'The gaff hook.' That, it appeared, was merely a snare for rabbiting. And the string tied to it? 'My client is not merely a surfing enthusiast, but a keen conservationist. Your Worships will be aware that the rabbits in this area are well known for their wide-ranging habits. He keeps the string on the snare in order not to cause the animal any additional cruelty while it awaits him coming to administer the *coup de grâce*.'

Ron and I were not sure what we were hearing. Nor did we understand quite what the lawyer was saying with such bland assurance about the Peter Tavy rabbits. But it didn't matter. Despite 'Gaffer' himself looking over to us with the sort of expression which said, apologetically, 'It was worth a try'; despite my almost pre-empting the magistrates' decision by writing the outcome into my notebook, there was still a surprise to come.

The worthy Justices trooped back with their usual air of virtuous self-importance. 'Not guilty,' said the Chairman as they sat down again after their retirement. And 'Not Guilty' was what I heard 'Gaffer' repeating to himself unbelievingly, as he sat afterwards, pint in hand, in the bar of the Bedford Hotel.

I am still waiting for the day when the local Tourist Board adds surfing to our list of inland attractions. Meanwhile, I would advise visitors to look out for their St Christopher medals. It is not beyond the bounds of possibility that anyone found searching for such a trinket in the River Tavy might find himself in court, on a poaching charge.

I have often pondered wherein lies the attraction of this kind of poaching. It is not necessarily easy work. You have to be up and about when more honest folk are safely abed. You have to brave unkindly weather, and long waits on cold river banks. You have to use your own car, for which you get neither mileage allowances nor tax relief. You have no regular pay-cheque nor assured income. You get neither sick pay nor holidays. And above all, you face the ever present possibility of being caught and (nowadays) being sent to gaol. So given that you need to have at least reasonable intelligence to understand the ways of the fish, and to organize yourself into taking and selling them illegally, you could well use such abilities in some other, legitimate occupation.

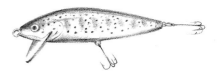

Rapala lure

So why do people become poachers? 'What you do for yourself isn't work,' said one local man. 'I could get a proper job tomorrow if I wanted one. I'm a skilled builder, see! But working regular like, for a boss, isn't for me. I don't want to be tied down; I want to come and go as I please and take on odd jobs when I want to. I look after the wife and kids and don't bother nobody, so where's the harm? And I don't take spawning salmon or damage the river. If all your proper fishermen were as I careful as I am, you'm bailiffs would have no trouble.'

And in this exceptional case, he was probably right. What he did had probably been done by his father before him, and by his grandfather before that, and his knowledge of fish and the rivers on which he preyed was almost certainly bred into him since childhood. In a sense, I was the intruder into this rural scene. He was the conservative and I was the radical, come to regulate what some might argue had, until forty years or so ago, almost regulated itself. Perhaps.

Late summer and early autumn, as the fish move upriver, is a
favourite time for poachers, and because we know where the fish
are likely to be as well as the poachers do, it is not a bad time for us
to capture them. At least on the river—as opposed to the estuary
where poachers can dissemble, or drop fish overboard, or escape
in a fast boat—we have a sporting chance of catching them in the

act, cutting off their potential escape routes and seizing the actual evidence of their misdeeds. Even if, as 'Gaffer' proved, this is not necessarily enough to secure a conviction.

I suppose we would all like to believe in poachers as 'proper' countrymen, often working on their own and taking no more than they need to keep their children in new shoes and themselves in a modest pint; cocking snooks at authority and the rich men who own stretches of water to which they feel they have their own rights. And there are still a few like that, even if most (especially those in the gangs which come from outside) are more villainous, and unpleasant.

One outsider who was harmless enough was 'Brummy' Johns. 'Brummy' came down most years from the Black Country for the summer sun, or a break from his importunate family. Sadly for him, 'Brummy' was a loser, the kind of petty villain who always gets caught while others go free. He was well known to us, and when we were tipped off that he had been seen on the Tavy, near the football field and within a mile of Tavistock town centre, we knew what he was after—a large 15 lb hen salmon lurking, with others, in a pool below where a supermarket trolley had lodged in a fish pass. The trolley seems a sad and unlikely obstruction in a salmon river, but the Tavy now flows through a modern town, not the abbey of five hundred years ago (were the monks litter conscious, I wonder?) and such hazards are all too common. We were used to such things.

Two local bad boys disappeared when we came to clear the trolley, but later the same day we had a telephone call to say that 'Brummy' was intent on taking this fish. Perhaps our informant was jealous of an outsider muscling in on his territory, or acted out of sheer ill-will; for among thieves, slights and dishonours are not uncommon. Whatever it was, we had our information and I agreed with a colleague, Harry de Quick, that we would conceal ourselves on the river bank in the expectation that 'Brummy' would appear on Sunday morning.

We made all our preparations on Saturday night when 'Brummy', following custom, was likely to be laying the found-ations of an expensive hangover in the Tavistock pubs. We made one 'hide' near the fish-pool and another near the next pool,

OPPOSITE

A poacher, complete with snare and salmon

Poacher-catcher at the
ready—a fellow bailiff
fully equipped in the bushes
beside the river

upstream, and arranged to meet with radios and binoculars before first light the following morning. Harry was to be in the upstream hide, and I in the lower. Everything, we liked to think, had been done according to what we imagined to be best SAS practice, camouflage nets and all.

We lay in our hides from 4.30 am until 8.30. It was rather less than the several days the SAS might be expected to lie-up elsewhere, but it was long enough for us. By the time we spotted 'Brummy' walking towards us over the football field, slapping his leg with a rolled-up Sunday newspaper, we had almost had enough. Suddenly, a pigeon rose noisily from a tree, and I thought that our cover would be blown. But 'Brummy' obviously thought his leg-slapping was the cause, and carried on until he was near the bank, ready for work. Carefully, he laid out his jacket and tobacco, put on his face mask and peered into the water where he imagined the fish to be, coming up to within three feet of me without noticing anything amiss. Even near the town, on a relatively well-used river bank, it is possible to conceal yourself successfully if you have the trick of lying completely still.

I watched every move 'Brummy' made as he solemnly selected just the right hazel stick, notched a neat 'V' in one end, and took some rabbit wire for a snare from a pocket in his old-fashioned underpants. The stick, often used in these parts, was simply to guide the snare over the head, or more commonly the tail of the fish. Once the snare was ready, the stick would be dropped. By now, 'Brummy' was so intent on taking his fish that I was able to sit up and ready myself to leap on him, without his even hearing me. I jumped on him just as he pulled out a furiously struggling salmon. I have never seen a man so surprised, and with little wonder. When someone a mere foot or two away materializes from nowhere the shock to the system must be considerable. Poor 'Brummy' could only roll a cigarette with shaking fingers and marvel at the percipience of the official tribe which opposed him. It took him some time, shaking his saddened head, to recover, and after he was subsequently fined £100 with costs, I never saw him again. Early-morning shocks, after a night's drinking, had clearly been too much for him.

Snares, I guess, are the poacher's preferred tool. Rods and nets and all the paraphernalia of the normal angler would be very conspicuous, but a bit of wire can be carried in a pocket while a stick, if one is needed, can be cut at the riverside. Kevin Hooley was a snare man, and an expert. I had known him for a long time, and even (grudgingly) admired his abilities, though I could hardly condone his activities. He was a long-term poacher, almost a professional, and I knew him to have taken many fine salmon. He had even, cheekily, sent me photographs of some of them, proudly displayed on the river bank, much as they might be after a laird's fishing party. But he never succeeded in fooling me better than when he took one huge $37^1/_2$-pounder straight past my suspicious nose.

He had seen a salmon near Ward Bridge on the Walkham, its head buried under the bank in the tangled roots of a large rhododendron. With the rabbit wire he had, he was unable to take such a big fish, so he had walked back to his car at the Dartmoor Inn near Merrivale and gone home to pick up some heavier duty wire. Parking inconspicuously among the customers' cars at Merrivale again, he went back to the pool, but failed to find his fish. Getting his accomplice to stone the pool above, he finally stirred it, managing to seize it by the head and hold it while it took off with him like a runaway horse.

Finally, he killed it, but it took both men, after stashing their wet suits, to carry it back to Merrivale. There only just in time, and from across the road, they saw my car. This was a disaster, but Hooley was equal to it. Spotting some bits of rusted iron lying about in the riding school opposite the inn, he sought and got the owner's permission to take away the scrap, having first laid the salmon in an ancient pig trough. Hooley then walked back to the car, greeted me cheerily and willingly stopped as I questioned him about what he was doing near one of our mutually favourite rivers. He was collecting scrap, he said, and to prove it, he took his car over to the riding school and in my full view, loaded the bits of iron, plus the old pig trough and its contents—namely, one $37^1/_2$ lb salmon—into the boot of his car.

I'm not sure what would have happened had I expressed an interest in the pig trough. Enough that I did not and only learned the story in the Peter Tavy Inn much later, by which time I was able to be philosophical about it. In truth, although I would have prosecuted him had I found him out at the time, the activities of Hooley and his ilk were not my main concern. Our main fish losses, and the greatest damage to salmon and to future stocks, came from the estuary poachers—compared with whom, the local river men were almost unimportant. These netters, sometimes taking anything up to fifty or sixty sea trout in one net-pass, were the bad guys, the people we really needed to arrest and keep arresting if salmon and sea trout fishing on our Devon rivers was to have a future.

One fine late-summer evening, on boat patrol of the Tamar estuary with another warden, we spotted some seven poachers taking advantage of a late run of sea trout. They all had small netting boats, and were probably opportunists rather than regular

OPPOSITE

Salmon leaping upstream
in an effort to reach the
breeding grounds

poachers. One, however, I recognized as a professional, using his 'amateur' friend as a look-out. We had to comport ourselves carefully, since at the first sight or sound of a warden's boat, the weighted old fertilizer bags holding their catches would be dumped over the side, with a string attached for later recovery.

For about an hour-and-a-half we watched and waited. We knew they had taken sea trout, but we needed to get into the right position with the sun behind us to drift down upon them unobserved. It was a bright evening, with the sun reflecting strongly on the water surface, making it difficult to look directly into. Or so we hoped.

Estuary netting boat

Our strategy worked. Cutting the engine, we drifted in on the tide towards the Tamar Bridge. Our adversaries noticed nothing, even the look-out being engrossed in his partner's work. Suddenly, from about fifty yards away, they saw us and realized who we were. It was time to act, our moment had come. Pointing the boat in the right direction, we slammed the engines on full and, with more enthusiasm than sense, attacked.

I can't remember how long it takes for a super-tanker to stop in mid-channel, but I know it's too long for the comfort of any ship in its way. And so it was, scaling down to the tiny boat which we used, with ours. At full speed, with my colleague standing in the bows like an avenging demon king, we inadvertently rammed the opposing boat amidships. I was untouched. Even the boat was not seriously damaged, and the poachers too escaped very lightly.

But my partner was less lucky. He, I fear, exited more than abruptly from his position of hands-on command. As our boat stopped, he continued on. In a graceful arc, he somersaulted out of the bows like Captain Thunder, the human cannonball, to land some yards away on a bag of stolen fish. It was an appropriate place to end up, and all things considered, he took his involuntary flight very well, and with some dignity. After all, it led to one arrest that not even the most brazen of poachers could protest.

Not all of the autumn was spent chasing poachers. Many of our days were passed routinely, walking upriver to check the spawning grounds for obstructions and pollution and to make sure that the cow-parsley had died back far enough to provide decent conditions for our returning travellers. After such a hazardous venture into the seas beyond Plymouth they deserved a decent welcome, although not even the Water Authority could guarantee river levels adequate for a smooth journey upstream.

My autumn diaries are filled with a lot of diverse visits and many notes of 'NTR'—'Nothing to Report'. I moved to different places almost every day—from the River Dart in the east, to the Launceston office in the north and the River Tamar in the west— filling the pages with records of farm inspections, routine fish surveys at Mill Hill, and planned and unplanned enforcement patrols in areas where poachers were known to work. We made several promising sorties against a couple of 'firms' of experienced fish stealers, all of which prove futile, and (as always) I spent many days touring the catchment areas simply to check that nothing untoward had happened there and to see that all was well in the smaller streams of the high moor.

The months vary, as do the days. But there is a loose pattern to our toil, and there were attempts to formalize the amounts of time we devoted to different activities. Obviously, these could not be written in stone, since so much of our work was subject to the unexpected that the best laid of our rationalization plans were always being thrown askew. One noble attempt to allocate available manpower (which was never really enough) produced a breakdown of activities roughly as follows (see page 99).

Tree studies
above w/bridge
Oct '90

20% Fisheries—to planned and unplanned enforcement patrols; hatchery duties and river management tasks; for example, trash, dams, gravels, fish farm inspections and so on.

8% Environmental—to assisting on fisheries surveys, and helping the new Roadford Reservoir team on trapping and survey work.

23% Pollution—assisting on farm inspections and coastal marine sampling.

36% Catchment Inspection—making routine 'multifunctional' patrols of catchment areas.

5% Water Licensing—visiting sites and answering queries.

7% Administration—including staff meetings, training and equipment maintenance.

In practice, the percentage of available manpower spent on these jobs varied according to the current levels of poaching in the area, the number of pollution incidents and much else unforeseeable, and not all wardens divided their individual time in these proportions, since the plan was designed to cover the activities of the workforce as a whole.

OPPOSITE

A page from my sketch book, of autumnal trees

I don't think our sternest critics could complain that we devoted too much time to sitting at desks. We had no desks, and most of our limited paper work was done at home, very often in our own time. Some hours had to be spent in meetings, if only for policy to be discussed, new procedures to be explained and common experiences shared more formally than in an off-duty pub. But most of our diaries would show that well over ninety per cent of our duty time was spent outdoors, on the ground, and very largely on catchment inspections.

Such duty time was not mindless. Arresting someone for poaching is arguably more tricky than arresting him for some other crime, since poachers can often appear innocent enough, wandering the woods with nothing more deadly than a hazel stick and a bag to hold their sandwiches. If we were ever to secure successful convictions, we needed to be very conversant with all the 'points to prove' and the right evidential procedures. We also needed to have a good working knowledge of fisheries and conservation legislation and the various orders made under this and other legislation. My files contain instructions on everything from health and safety at work to advice on the killing of cormorants and herons, the operation of radios and the checking of water abstraction licence-holders. We remained, however, creatures of the outdoors, and the weather.

Only a genius, with a direct line to the elements could predict our West Devon weather with any great certainty. I suppose it is little different from that of the rest of Britain, a bit warmer and wetter perhaps, less prone to biting winds than the east coast, and possibly more inconstant. But even within this small district, it is dangerous to generalize about it. Tavistock can be fine and sunny while ten miles away, over the moors, fog covers the hills in damp grey shrouds. At this time of the year, you can never be sure whether the climate of the day will exhilarate or depress you, and if you are a bailiff, duty-bound to a trip to Tavy Cleave or the Upper Dart, you are well advised to treat all forecasts with great caution. Trust in the gods, by all means, but keep some dry socks and a waterproof in the back of your car.

Salmon spear

By late autumn, some fish may still be stuck in low pools, or crouched in underhangs for lack of water to move upwards. Then, in a great burst, clouds will break on the moor and the deluge will run off the hills into the upland streams. Within days, the river levels will rise and the salmon which despaired of moving will find itself battling against a fast-running torrent. When the Tavy shows its flooded teeth, it can be frightening; more like the product of wild mountains than tors which stand, at most, a mere three thousand feet above sea-level. People lean over the bridge and marvel at the river's power, as bushes and sometimes trees are swept downstream in furious maelstrom. Anxious mothers draw back their children from the edge of the bankside path and even water-conditioned labradors shy away from the boiling spray.

At this time, there is nothing much for a bailiff to do except hope that the fish passes will not be damaged, nor the upstream gravels disturbed by the howling flood. We know that the water

Men fishing from the top of Horrabridge

will disappear almost as quickly as it comes, and we can only wait for the river to settle back to its gentler self, so that we can assess the depredations and check what has happened to those fish that were waiting for the chance to move on. Perhaps they got more water than they needed: when the river is in this state I often wonder how any creature can survive in it, much less move upwards against the current. But they do, and I am soon back in business. As the fish begin to move again, so do our opponents.

The snare, I wrote earlier, is one much favoured tool of local poachers. Another is the snatch, a largish, heavily-weighted, triple hook which is rather more difficult to conceal, or explain away if someone is found carrying it through the woods, late at night. To use it, a poacher will normally have a shrewd idea where his chosen salmon is lying. He'll then approach after dark and transfix his fish in the beam of a powerful torch. Lowering his hook into position just beneath the fish, he then 'snatches' upwards and takes his prey. It's an efficient way to take a salmon illegally, but it does leave very obvious marks, so that the poacher may have a problem in disposing of it.

In the old days, I suspect that more than half of all the illegally-taken fish were sold at back doors, and that many a formal dinner party (or smart restaurant table) was graced by salmon which were poached before they were grilled. Now, my guess is that a large part of the large-scale poachers' hauls are sold on the Continent, and that even some successful individual poachers must use this market.

In an ideal world, poaching would disappear and the bailiff-as-policeman would become redundant. River wardens would work only on fish conservation and river improvement, and all rivers and estuaries would be open to all men to fish as they will, except with nets. Even now, in New Zealand and parts of Canada, fish are so plentiful and people so few that bailiffs are hardly needed. I remember on a trip to Vancouver marvelling at the wealth of trout that almost fell over themselves in their rush to self-destruction. Had I travelled further inland, I might have found even more and bigger fish, with no one to deny my right to catch and kill them.

Sadly, such rights (if they ever existed) have everywhere disappeared from the British Isles (although they still survive in limited form in western Ireland), and even children have trouble finding somewhere to try out their prized, first rods. The old South West Water Authority sensibly made permits available, at low fees, to enable children to fish the Tavy where it flowed through Tavistock town, and even stocked fish for their benefit. But such 'free' reaches are rare and becoming rarer. Budding fishermen of the future are unlikely to find anywhere to learn and practise their art outside a lake fishery—unless, of course, their fathers are poachers, or rich enough to rent them a stretch on a trout stream.

Such sombre thoughts go with the dying days of autumn. Everything now is winding down towards the year's end. Visiting fishermen depart and tourists desert the caravan parks, although not quite so quickly as they once did. Over the past few years, the holiday season has begun to expand at both ends, and even well into October the shutters have not all been closed. By November, however, the knell of passing summer is truly sounded. Damp mists have rolled in, most of the migratory birds have disappeared and the woods round Grenofen are walked only by a few hardy local dog owners. Only the joy of the avocets starting to arrive back on the Tamar estuary relieves the prevailing grey. Ironically, for they themselves feed on small fish and marine creatures, these beautiful birds were once slaughtered to make fishing flies of their feathers. Now, they are deservedly protected, to lighten the day of any bailiff lucky enough to be working on the late-autumn estuary, and any artist who can find the time to paint them.

The official salmon season may now be over, but we are still busy on arduous patrolling of the rivers' upper reaches. About now, the sea trout will begin to arrive for spawning, to be followed by salmon towards the end of the month, and we must get into practice to begin counting the redds. This is an annual task, undertaken to draw up a spawning map which will help the Authority to see what is happening in the river system, and to monitor any year-to-year changes. And despite the prevailing murk, it was a job I enjoyed doing. Research, despite the scepticism of some of the older hands, is vital to angling's future, and helping with it was for me a welcome and positive change from the negative catching of small-time poachers. But of this, more in the pages that follow, when I come to December and the brighter days that go with early frost.

Detail of a salmon tail

CHAPTER FOUR

WEST COUNTRY WINTER

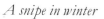

A snipe in winter

Contrary to cynical opinion, bailiffs do not hibernate. Even in the bleakest of Dartmoor midwinters, when the earth is as hard as iron, the rivers rarely turn to stone. Somewhere below the cold surface, life goes on, and we must monitor it. While sensible anglers are at home in front of warm fires, reading a Robin Armstrong book, the guardians of their heritage will be walking the Tavy, or messing about on the estuary in a small boat and a very keen wind. December through February, even in a part of Britain said to be milder than most, is not warm, especially when the air is howling in from the east and one is working on the upper reaches of a moorland stream, checking that the redds have not been disturbed by storm or vandal.

The secret of a comfortable outdoor life is proper clothes. Not necessarily huge thick coats, but sensible layers of wool which are warm without being constricting, and a waterproof outer anorak to keep out the wind and the wet. Good thermal socks, stout boots and a hat are essential; forget the proper hat and you effectively lose a quarter of all the heat you generate, like leaving the front door open when the fire's on in the living-room. However cold the winter moor, you can be quite comfortable provided you wear the right things, keep dry and continue to think of your pay-cheque.

I actually enjoy the winter. It is not the worst of seasons, but just a different one. There is never a month in England when at least one day is not clearer and brighter and fresher than any day anywhere else, and I would not change things for perpetual sunshine and endless reliable weeks with neither rain nor chill. To live under eternally blue skies must surely render one insensate to the wonderful variety of the natural world, and it is hardly surprising if beach bums, anaesthetized by ultra-violet rays, are not noted for their contributions to man's advancement. Or so I told myself when called out one winter midnight.

We had heard that illegal netsmen were active on the estuary, despite our having confiscated some thirty-two monofilament nets in the previous few weeks in the Plym estuary alone. The nets themselves are worth several thousand pounds. Add the cost of boats, engines and the rest and the value of the fish taken illegally becomes apparent. Such an amount of criminal capital is not laid out without hope of very large returns, probably from sales made on the Continent, where salmon make much more than they do here and fewer questions are likely to be asked about their provenance.

Our job was to frustrate these hopes, which is why I found myself in a small boat on the Plym estuary in the middle of the night, steadying myself against the movement induced by a heavy swell and wishing I was safely in bed. The sea was dark and foreboding. Going slowly, the bow ploughed into it with a series of heavy thwacks which led me to wonder when it would split open. The water seemed very close and cold; the shore further away than it actually was. On land, people were warmly wrapped before a fire, or peacefully sleeping, while I tried to pretend to being action man—the lean, keen hero of South West Water's Special Boat Section (Bailiff's Branch).

Alas, no such Section exists, nor was there any particular glamour attached to this work. It was simply part of our normal job. Yet poking about in the chilly December dark, with nothing between us and the sombre deep except the thin shell of an outboard-engined, 14-foot boat, is by any occupational standards a daunting experience. It was as well that Ron, my colleague on this patrol, knew about small boats and was at home on the water.

By half past two, with the night blacker and bleaker than ever, we moved out of Plymouth's Sutton Harbour towards the inner

The elegant head of a curlew

breakwater off Mountbatten Point. Here, a lifetime ago, T. E. Lawrence served as Aircraftman Shaw on the Royal Air Force station that was subsequently home to flying boats protecting wartime convoys. I am told it was considered a good posting, offering plenty of scope to those who liked the sea and the countryside, but close enough for less ascetic servicemen than Lawrence to enjoy the wealth of Union Street's infamous pubs, clubs and other, more dubious delights.

From Plymouth Sound's outer breakwater, in a line due north to the shore below the magnificent old fort (which still houses today's Royal Marines) on the eastern side of the Hoe, is about two miles. At that point, the water is some three miles across, narrowing as one comes inshore. It constitutes a lot of sea, with plenty of movement in it, and even as we ploughed out towards Mountbatten Point, only a quarter mile or so away, it became decidedly lumpy. Putting discretion firmly before valour, we turned towards the relative calm of Cattewater, the mouth of the River Plym, and worked our way upriver among the moored yachts towards Laira Bridge, which carries the traffic between the city and the coastal resorts of South Devon. In this piece of water, the Harbour Commissioners had banned all nets, so that any we found must be illegal. But searching among all the buoys and yachts was difficult, and only by the most fortunate chance were we likely to score a success. That night, we found nothing.

Ron, however, was keen to find evidence of something. He had made the struggle against illegal netting almost into a personal campaign, and was eager to extend our patrol beyond the Mountbatten breakwater. By then, it was after 4 am, and still very dark. The sea had eased slightly, but I had no confidence that it would not change, and very quickly, from tolerable to very rough. We pressed on, moving seawards so as to have the shore-lights in front of us when we came to look for nets. Soon, we were in Jennycliff Bay, with the swell running strongly, and every prospect of a nasty return trip as the wind backed and began to blow from off-shore. The large ships anchored within the outer breakwater were rolling perceptibly, but not as sickeningly as we, and they certainly afforded much more protection to their crew than our small cuddy gave to us. As we corkscrewed our way through the water, taking care to skirt the white waves surrounding an old wreck, I gave thanks that I had a strong stomach.

Here, if anywhere, we might have found nets, but we could not go too far inshore in these conditions lest we ended up on the rocks. Judging distance in the dark is not easy, shoreline reference points are hard to distinguish and the black water cannot readily be estimated by mentally chopping it up into football or cricket pitch lengths. Ron, unusually, played very safe, taking no chances. Even so, we got close to the shore, going slowly between the

Female goosander

The Tavy estuary

crab-pots and keeping a wary eye open for high-set nets which might foul our tiny propeller. Those few small blades of turned brass were our lifeline, and that they so reliably sped us forward against tide and wind was a minor miracle.

By an oversight we had no big lamp to probe our way through the darkness, so we navigated by instinct back to the security of the inner breakwater. The sea was still heavy and we bounced alarmingly on our final run across the bay but made the safety of Sutton Harbour in good order. I went ashore to a cup of hot coffee feeling heroic, but knowing that our mission, if it can be called that, had been unsuccessful. We knew that illegal netting took place in the area we had been searching, but we could not prove it. For the time being, we could only let the poachers know that we were aware of their activities. This we did by surreptitiously examining a few suspected boats and leaving the nets in a position conspicuously different from where we found them. This, we hoped, might warn off some villains, although I personally doubted it. The stakes were too big for a gentle reminder of our presence to have any effect other than to make the villains even more careful.

The night was creeping towards dawn by the time I collected my car and made my way home. Stopping at Grenofen for signs of any activity, I found nothing other than litter that might have been left by some courting couple (a term still used in these old-fashioned parts). Going slightly out of my way, I called at Abbey Bridge in Tavistock, but here, too, all was well. Friday traders were dressing their stalls for the penultimate market before Christmas, while houses and shops still slept. Near the centre, the town presented an early-morning picture of friendly bustle—no place, one might think, for criminal enterprise to flourish; yet criminal enterprise was just what I had spent the night trying to foil.

As a watery sun rose above the tors to the east, I made my way home across the deserted public golf course and the fringes of the moor. Although my work brought many frustrations and wasted nights, it also offered, among many pleasures, the quiet joy of driving along country lanes when most of the world was still asleep. But if most of West Country humankind was not yet awake, the natural world was. People in cultures which believe that trees and plants have souls would have found my drive confirming their faith. On that particular cold, quiet winter morning, even a sceptical water bailiff could feel 'a presence that', as Wordsworth put it, 'disturbs … a sense sublime, of something far more deeply interfused' with this Devon world than a mere arrangement of inanimate rocks and moorland.

*Statue of Sir Francis
Drake at Tavistock*

Here on Dartmoor, where hut circles still outline the evidence of early man, and the forbidding land was fashioned by eruptions beyond our imagining, they say that at midnight on Christmas Eve, cattle and sheep will turn and kneel towards Bethlehem, in acknowledgement of the birth of the Christ-child. The Dorset oxen of Hardy's day were said to do the same, and I have never spoilt the story by trying to verify it. But I don't find it at all hard to believe that our patient cattle, and our small, heavy-coated Dartmoor ponies, foraging stoically for their sparse winter commons, know much more about the order of heaven and earth than we do.

Robin Armstrong

I arrived at Woodtown tired and thoughtful. There had been no 'lampers' at Grenofen looking for the late-coming salmon that spawn in the middle reaches of the river and known here as 'greenbacks', nor any sign of poachers near the town. Perhaps our enemy had declared a Christmas truce, though I thought it unlikely. The poachers we faced were hardly that sort, although some, even the hard ones, could sometimes make us smile, as the Black brothers did after a winter night on the River Meavy.

It was two o'clock in the morning when I received the telephone call. At that time, the voice on the other end of the line is either agitated, which betokens an informant speaking directly, or cool and calm, which means a policeman, perhaps relaying a message from someone else. This time it was the Water Authority's main control in Exeter, to say they had had a call advising them, somewhat clumsily, of 'a poaching incident which was about to take place'. In other words, a call from an informer with inside knowledge.

I dislike the word 'snout' but that was what this man was, and possibly still is. If such people did not exist, our work would be less productive. West Devon covers a very large area, and without occasional snippets of information, we should rarely catch or deter anybody. Successful policing of any kind demands 'good intelligence', and this man (for I had guessed who he was) was a source on whom I could rely. I rang him back. His number, nowhere written down on paper, for his safety and my interests, was etched in my mind and I got through to him straightaway.

'What's going on?' I asked. The adrenalin was already flowing, and I was wide awake.

It was a group which I shall call, for their peace and mine, the Black brothers, and they would be there now, he said, specifying a particular place on a river about twelve miles away. He would stake his reputation on it, and since he had never let me down in the past, I took him at his word. But the mention of these brothers made me wary. One of them, large and menacing, was intimidating not only physically but in other ways. He was certainly not someone I would like to accost alone, on a dark night, so I decided to seek assistance.

First I got Ray, a new but knowledgeable colleague, to join me

OPPOSITE

The majestic tracery of a chestnut in winter, with a squirrel's dray in its upper branches

A poacher by night in the cold of winter

and then I rang the police. When violence is on the cards, it is always best to have a uniformed man on hand, and the police never object to assisting in such cases. The poachers often turn out to be people whom the police suspect of other crimes, and the Black brothers, one of whom had recently been concerned in a case where he had ineptly dropped a stolen safe on his foot, were very much in that category.

People accused of poaching react in different ways. Some reconcile themselves to the inevitable; many bluster and deny the charge and a small minority threaten violence against their accuser. Faced by the last, I simply point out that the case is about a fish, not a murder. And usually, things go no further. But with the

Black brothers, I wasn't sure how well my approach would be received.

I knew where they would be, and I had a good idea where they would try to hide their car. I also knew, from a visit the previous day, that the river would probably be high and running strongly, and anyone trying to take fish there would find it difficult. Even so, I couldn't afford not to go out. If the brothers thought there was any chance that we had relaxed, they would try for something, whatever the state of the water. So I continued to get ready— clothes on top of pyjamas; watch; whistle; radio; night-sight and pocket tape-recorder for note taking. I was organized and prepared.

We met the police as arranged and briefed them on what we knew of the Blacks' methods. Usually one of the brothers, Big Bill, trying hard to look innocent, would be sent ahead of the others, carrying none of the poacher's usual gear. If the coast was clear and all seemed well, he would then summon his fellows. Tonight, though, black though it was, he spotted us. With the breaking of the storm which had been threatening since we came out, spectacular flashes of lightning had suddenly lit up the Stygian night like a series of Army flares, and Big Bill came virtuously out of the darkness. The lightning must have rendered us visible over half the county. Our ambush was clearly foiled, and by the time Big Bill reached us the other brothers were either in hiding or miles away over the fields. Big Bill, secure in the knowledge that he had nothing incriminating on him, was coming back to pick up their battered car.

'I was a bit concerned,' he said. 'I thought me car might have been vandalized.'

Even vandals, I thought to myself, would have been hard pressed to make the car more awful than it already was.

Ray and I then decided to search the field where we had first seen Big Bill. We found nothing, so while we waited for a police dog and handler, Bill regaled our policeman with gossip about his family. He was smiling, confident that he had escaped charges but not too confident about the trouble he'd get from his wife if she heard that he came back late. He was also concerned about his son.

'The boy's getting a bit heavy,' he explained. 'Real violent. I'm

Bill Black—a colourful character

quite worried about him. Especially as the wife's just gone into hospital with a tropical pregnancy.' I think he meant 'entropic', but I wasn't going to argue.

'Seventeen stone and full of mischief,' he went on with some pride. But the policeman had had enough of Bill's wife, whatever her size. It was the son who concerned him.

'What about this lad of yours,' said our conscientious bobby. 'In what way is he violent?'

'Well!' said Bill. 'He's started nutting people, especially me.'

'You must stop him now,' said the constable, visualizing the future delinquent. 'How old is he? Is it too late to talk to him about it?'

'Perhaps it is,' Bill replied, shaking his head sadly. 'Perhaps it is. He's already gone ten months.'

After that, the rest of the night was something of an anti-climax. We searched hard, but found nought. The dog and its handler departed, and we went back to my kitchen. We left Big Bill in ebullient mood, but I didn't consider the night a total defeat as I might once have done, when early enthusiasm demanded constant results. Despite the fruitless outcome, I was content that we had learned something—in future, we would be much more wary of thunderstorms. Had it not been for the lightning disclosing our presence, we might have been more successful. And Big Bill's seventeen-stone wife, finding him arrested, might have become more angry with him than she no doubt already was.

The Meavy is not a river on which I often worked, although I knew it fairly well. It's different from the Tavy, being more subdued and less volatile, because its flow is to some degree controlled by the dam leading from Burrator Reservoir at its northern source. For much of its length, it meanders through woods and pasture land as though, in places, it were some up-country and upmarket chalk stream rather than an uncouth product of the moors. It is also fairly easy to walk. In one part, where it flows through a shoot, overgrown banks have actually been cleared and trimmed, as though it were aspiring to be fished by men in brogues made by Mr Lobb, with chauffeur-driven cars waiting to take them back to the London flight from Plymouth airport. Yet it never quite succeeds in living up to this image. In this part of the world, no river is entirely well mannered and domesticated.

I quite liked the Meavy, even though it was out of the common run of most of my streams; its surface often being covered in rich weed quite unlike anything one sees on the Tavy, or the Dart. But I rarely had time to see it much in summer, looking upon it as a river that comes into its own in winter as a splendid spawning river. For those fish that successfully got through the illegal nets in the estuary, its gravels made fine redds, which one can inspect more easily than most of those further up on the high moor. Because of this, and also because I enjoy studying and painting the

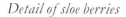

Detail of sloe berries

fascinating shapes and forms which make up the root systems below its many overhangs, I like going there in winter, when nothing much else stirs but the local poachers.

Since Meavy salmon arrive late and spawn quickly, often in the tails of the pools where the beds may be covered in only six to eight inches of water, they present tempting targets to those who know the river well. In the days before the onus of proving a fish was received in good faith was placed on the recipient, the use of lamps, spears and snares were popular poaching techniques. Simply shine a torch into the water where the fish are known to lurk, catch them in the beam of light and bring a wire snare gently over their heads until you can jerk hard and capture them. The alternative is to spear them, but both methods leave marks which show them to have been poached, rather than caught legitimately with rod and line.

The Black brothers had come for salmon, or rather for the money which salmon represented, and I doubt if they ever gave any thought to the diversity of a universe which produced such a mysterious fish. And why should they? In the limited world in which they lived and moved, with poverty an ever-present guest and fresh financial disasters awaiting round every corner, it is unlikely that philosophic discourse on the evolution of fish took up much of their spare-time. They might know, indeed they certainly did know, the whereabouts of the best lies and the most productive pools and the best ways to winkle fish out of them, but beyond that, their knowledge did not extend. Their world was small and limited, beginning and ending within about thirty miles of where they lived. But they do know something about fish and fishing.

Even they, however, can tell us nothing new about the wayward journeyings of the Atlantic salmon, and nor, except in broad brushstrokes, can all the erudite authors in the world. Dozens of volumes have been written about catching salmon, but what the writers (or even bailiffs) really know about a salmon's life outside its home river is largely conjectural. And so, I shall stick to spawning, of which bailiffs do have some experience.

Salmon or the salmon egg, which comes first? Starting at the mouth of the home river, with fish that have successfully escaped the estuary netsmen, returning salmon still face many hazards. Middle-river poachers and legitimate anglers, low water and spates, weirs and fish-passes all represent obstacles which can be difficult to overcome. In West Devon, fish have a long way to travel up a sometimes inhospitable stream before they reach the spawning grounds. But once arrived there, all troubles are forgotten (I suspect) as natural urges take command. The female will decide where in the gravels she will hollow out a redd in which to lay her eggs without losing all of them. The male, hovering close by like an excited voyeur, will then cover the eggs with his milt, and conception, on a rather larger than human-life scale, will follow. The only part which bailiffs play in the wasteful accouchement (for most eggs are lost, or eaten) is to see beforehand that the gravels are clean and free from weed and that, as far as possible, nothing is present to mar the joys of successful mating.

What the parent fish get out of this near virginal sex is not known to fish psychologists nor anyone else, but the process leaves them fairly exhausted. Having, in the cheap argot of another sport, 'done the business', both parties stagger back as best they can to the sea. Bearing in mind that they have not really eaten since coming in to the fresh water, these kelts, as they are now called, are thin and exhausted. What flesh they have is flabby, and if, though it is against the law, you were to catch one and eat it, you would find it distinctly short on flavour. Most kelts, indeed, have but a short time to live. Few cock fish reach the sea again, and many hen fish also fail to survive the return journey. Those strong ones that do, however, seem to be reborn. They may come back to the same river three or four times, growing bigger (though not sweeter in the flesh) each time.

While the parents, or many of them, are making the supreme sacrifice, the fertilized eggs are steadily developing in their redds. How long they take to hatch depends on many factors, such as water temperature, the amount of oxygen in the water, even the number of spates they experience. But most will emerge as tiny fish in February. Meanwhile, the redds will have been frequently checked by patrolling bailiffs, to ensure that they remain undisturbed by curious man or straying beast.

Mostly for two, but sometimes for up to three years, these newly hatched fish remain in the river, behaving like the small trout with which they are often confused, and struggling for food in a relatively barren environment. Our rivers in West Devon are not exactly insect rich, and no fish here has an easy upbringing. With luck, however, when they have grown to about six inches long, and become entitled to call themselves smolt, they will make the dangerous migration to the sea. This is when we lose track of them. Nobody, yet, knows with certainty exactly where they go, nor why, although they're thought to travel far into the Atlantic. Wherever they go, they must feed richly from some vast ocean larder, since in the two or three years they are away from the place of their birth, they grow to be anything between four to twelve pounds.

It must be a shock for them, returning for the first time as grilse, to exchange the rich regime of the ocean for the fasting which they undertake on coming back to fresh water. So long as they are away from the ocean, they eat nothing except for an occasional fly—taken fairly unenthusiastically, and more out of habit than for food—since their digestive systems are believed to have atrophied before they even enter their home rivers.

Some fish ('springers') will arrive early, most will come by summer and other fish ('greenbacks') will come late. There is rarely a time when something is not moving somewhere in the river system, nor when some aberrant fish is not confounding the natural order of things. Every time we try to classify different fish into different months, or try to put a date to the end of spawning, we are confounded by an exception. One February a local fishing enthusiast brought me the carcass of a huge sea trout which he had found floating in the tail of a pool on the River Walkham. It was not a kelt, but a freshly returning fish that had died of injury or disease, and at $16\frac{1}{2}$ lb was the biggest I had ever seen on that river. It proved to me that although there are clear differences between one part of the year and another, a bailiff should never be surprised by the unexpected.

But back to spawning, and the part the river warden plays in seeing that it takes place successfully. It would be nice to see ourselves in the role of midwives, vital attendants at the King of

OPPOSITE
A woodcock lies well camouflaged in its nest

Robin Armstrong '86

Pollarded trees are sometimes used to hide stolen salmon

the River's delicate delivery, but in fact there is not much we can do to ensure that the actual conception and subsequent births go well. We check and count the redds, which is never an easy task, since it is hard to spot them in the first place, and even harder to distinguish between those of salmon and those of sea trout (although sea trout mostly turn to smaller stones than salmon). And sometimes, showing off our knowledge of the river, we introduce some wide-eyed visitor to the miracle going on beneath the cold waters; the uninitiated, trying to find redds without a live guide, is likely to be disappointed.

Perhaps one day scientists will be able to tell us why particular rivers are chosen as spawning grounds and others are not, but not yet. Spawning remains one of nature's many mysteries, just as dark as the puzzle of the salmon's peregrinations in the Atlantic. Running into the Tavy near my cottage, for example, a small stream called the Penny-Come-Quick (I am not sure why) offers theoretically perfect gravel in which I would expect even the most fastidious salmon to rejoice. But far from blessing the gods for such a gift, and using it in their dozens, they avoid the place with an enthusiasm bordering on the macabre. In all the years I have walked the length of this small brook, hoping to see at least one kelt disporting there, I never have. Whether it is the water, its rate of flow, the spirits of the trees surrounding it or just sheer cussedness on the part of the fish themselves, I do not know. As it is, salmon in plenty continue to use the main stream, and short of forcibly diverting them into what I would consider is the better hole, I can only observe their behaviour and paint, as well as I can, the beauty that I am lucky enough to see.

Underwater painting sounds like something which people do in groups for Comic Relief, or alone, in the hope of achieving brief avant-garde fame through an Exhibition at the Tate. It conjures up visions of artists in swimming smocks and velvet berets, with wild looks in their eyes and paint brushes held between their teeth, chasing after nude models. It's the kind of subject you might find listed among the therapies of an expensive health farm, or the offerings of a loony Council's evening classes, but not in the index of a fishing book.

And yet, since fish (making a rough allowance for time engaged in leaping) spend all but about .001 per cent of their lives under water, a fish painter must make some effort to find out what his subjects look like in their native element. So although I don't actually paint under water, I do need to look at fish when they are under water, and to see their surroundings from an underwater perspective.

Spawning salmon

This is less easy than it may seem. You can stand in the main street of Stockbridge and watch trout gliding in and out of the culvert beneath the main road and think you have captured the essence of fish life. But you have not. What you see in these artificial circumstances is only a small part of the truth. To get the right picture of what a fish looks like in its home stream, with the water running between boulders and weed, and the sunlight striking it at different angles at different parts of the day, you need a view of your subject which is close and real and natural. And to get this, you must be prepared to spend long hours waiting until your chosen subject comes within proper sight.

Watching and making rough sketches at the same time is difficult—especially in winter. I am therefore doubly lucky to have had a friend with experience in an underwater search unit to supplement my own observations with a series of excellent photographs taken as he swam and walked below the surface moving upstream from Ward Bridge on the Walkham, just below my cottage. They are invaluable for reference. But I still need to see fish for myself, and for this I use a sort of reverse, home-made periscope, which I put together from mirrors and a plastic tube, about five feet long and some eight inches in diameter. It's not the most beautiful of artefacts, but it works.

As with anything remotely connected with fishing, or bird and animal watching, patience is needed to use the periscope. I usually employed it in reaches of clear water, standing in the shallows near known lies and holding one end under the surface while trying to make notes as best I could with the other hand. Managing this juggling act takes quite a bit of practice, especially on cold January days when fingers go numb. Yet one of my favourite paintings would have been impossible without the trusty periscope. During a winter walk along the Walkham River, I spotted two Atlantic salmon in the act of spawning. No wildlife artist could have failed to be inspired by such a sight, and I watched and sketched them as close up as I dared. Hurrying home, I made straight for the studio, took the largest sheet of hand-made paper I had in stock, and quickly pencil-sketched what I proposed to do. Then I stretched the paper in a plastic tray of clean water for some five or six hours before following this up with several water-colour washes. Then the picture was built up with pencil work, more water-colour and gouache. Again I worked on the detail of the stones, put the paper back to soak, and repeated the process, working on it until it built up into the diffused as well as detailed effect I had seen through the periscope. I am always excited by the effect obtained by deliber-ately diffusing the edge of an image, whether this is the main subject or some ancillary object, such as a stone or strand of weed. It always adds a new element to the completed painting.

The sight of salmon spawning is as magnificent as anything one can see on a river, apart perhaps from the sun-lit leaping of a huge fish over a weir. It deserves the grandest treatment one can give it, and in this case I was determined to re-create every majestic detail. In the end, I had a picture of 45 inches × 35 inches, one of the largest I have ever painted, and one which gave me as much satisfaction as I have ever known. When I finished the painting, I felt I had indeed managed to capture in some degree the wonderful mystery of the salmon's elemental begetting.

Leaving Devon for a few days to help a friend remove pike from the Kennet, I find that fishing a chalk stream of such stature in winter is a fascinating exercise. The open and leisurely Hampshire of the warm summer, with people sitting at tables outside and lounging on the banks in bright finery, has withdrawn behind tight-closed windows, into rooms with log fires. The doors of the pubs (essential adjuncts to all fishing expeditions) are kept shut behind customers who rush in, heavily clothed, to talk about burst pipes. But sport on the river is still good. The fishing is not difficult, and provided one is well wrapped up, it can be exhilarating to be out and about when others are sitting stuffily inside. It also provides a welcome change from patrolling, often fruitlessly, the even chillier waters of a Cornish estuary. I enjoy my break.

The realities of country life are somewhat removed from the idylls shown in the pages of the colour supplements. Ill-tempered villains and hard men are found in rural areas as well as towns, and I have no illusions about some of our younger poachers. I confess, however, to a sneaking regard for one or two of the older ones, several of whom have their own pride and sense of what is fitting. One, among a few who keep careful notes of their catches, meticulously records every detail of his criminal excursions, writing up his fishing diary with all the care of the owner of a great estate. And to some degree, I suppose, he regards our local rivers as his estate, even if he has no title to the freehold nor any right (in the eyes of the law) to the fish in them. I have only been allowed to glimpse part of his treasured notebooks, but that glimpse alone convinced me that as a record of wind and weather, river-state, condition of fish and the special circumstances in which he took them, his entries more than matched in breadth and interest those in the most expensive game books. Someday, I hope, he might let me illustrate them.

He is not the only poacher who is genuinely interested in the ways of fish. One old adversary, now retired from the river bank (or so he claims), recently sent me an intriguing and very personal account of 'greenbacks', the fish which come late and spawn early on several of our rivers, but particularly the Meavy. Since these observations are based on some twenty years' local experience,

Some winter studies, Roe deer,
fox track in the snow.
Redwing and dipper, both
fluffed up to insulate them
from the cold.

Robin Armstrong - Woodtown '91

they merit attention. My correspondent, to whom for obvious reasons I can accord no public credit, claims that these fish are also found on the Dart, Teign and Walkham, but his first one, a thirty-pounder, was caught in late November, about the year 1973, at Hill Bridge on the Tavy. 'It was,' he writes, 'the best example of a salmon I have ever seen, as it was fresh from the sea, and it put up quite an astonishing fight.'

Some four years later, he met a host of similar-looking fish, but this time in April, in the lower part of the Tavy near Bere Alston. He counted about sixteen of them, 'trapped in a small pool through lack of water ... darting about all over the place', in a manner he thought 'unusual'. Not unnaturally, since he knew these fish were neither kelts nor baggits (salmon that are in spawn), he initially thought they were 'springers'. But although they were in first-class condition, he felt there was something odd about them. They were restless; they seemed to sense that the river was about to rise, and a few days later, when it did, they disappeared very quickly. After scouring the river, in his words, 'for possibly the next thirty days, I did not find a single fish'. Again he naturally concluded that on finding there was not enough water to get upstream to spawn, the fish had returned to the sea.

Later experience convinced him he was wrong. He now believes, in his own words, 'beyond all shadow of doubt that these fish were greenback kelt and had already spawned the previous November, four to five months past, and were trapped in the river through an unusual lack of water, even though they were in excellent condition, much better than a "springer" that had been in the river for a couple of months.' To back up his argument, he recalls that later, and in different years, he once encountered a 10 lb greenback salmon in February, high up on the Tavy, in superb condition and 'moving so quickly that I lost sight of it almost immediately': others, of which he actually caught about twenty, he came across in November. The condition of the fish left him in no doubt that anglers catching early fish in February and March are not catching 'springers' but 'greenbacks', even though they are not aware of the fact. 'Because unlike "springers", "greenbacks" simply do not deteriorate in rivers, I am convinced that these are a distinct type or even race of salmon, as Mr King says.'

And who is Mr King? Mr G. M. King, although I have yet to confirm this, was apparently the author of an article on greenback salmon in the March 1956 edition of *The Field*. I don't know whether my correspondent keeps copies of this journal bound in leather, as one might expect to find in the quiet library of a gentleman's club, to be browsed over to the accompaniment of a large whisky, but it would be nice to think that he did. Meanwhile, it is reassuring to record that at least one zoologist *manqué* is alive and thriving among our local (retired) poachers. I am sure that the shade of Frederick Halford, who frequently wrote for *The Field*, would not disapprove.

The common frog

CHAPTER FIVE

CLOUDED WATERS

Snowdrops in flower

Towards the end of February, give or take a week or so, the spawning is over. The bailiff's year draws to its natural close, and he must ready himself once more for the start of another trout and salmon life-cycle. Whatever his geographical origins, in tiny hamlet or crowded inner-city, the best kind of river warden will have grown into a true countryman, ordering his life by the seasons and marking the passage of the months by nature's changes and the jobs to be done rather than by the calendar. Over the years, he will have become something more than a mere security man, or a technician. It will not be enough that he has learnt the rules of evidence, or the names given to a salmon at different stages of its life-cycle. Unless he has cultivated a deep and practical (never a romantic) love of nature, a feel for country ways, and an instinct that helps him distinguish between the genuine birdwatcher and the potential poacher, reconnoitring the ground with a view to later villainy, he is unlikely to be good at his job. Like an antique dealer who has a 'nose' for that which is genuine and that which is fake, he must learn to tell at a glance when the fish in a particular river are beginning to behave oddly, or the river itself is beginning to run 'wrong'.

These talents are nurtured by experience, but not everyone can acquire them. I cannot claim that one is born to be a bailiff, since I certainly was not, being very much bred of the city, and London at that. But somewhere beneath my urban skin, there must have been a hankering for greener pastures and rural freedoms, since I ran away to become a gamekeeper (without much knowing what a gamekeeper was or did) when I was fifteen, and had begun to teach myself fishing and learn about wildlife well before that.

The gamekeeping was not a success, and I turned to another love, apprenticing myself to the trade of artist. I use the word 'trade' deliberately, because it implies 'craft', and I have much respect for craftsmen. A good fisherman is a craftsman. So, too, is a good bailiff. Both need the kind of skill that cannot be gained without patient study and long practice, and both must be ready to acknowledge that there is never any end to what they can learn. Even now, after over thirty-five years on various river banks and sea-shores, I keep meeting people who have some new, useful tip to offer me.

And so with the people I met during my bailiff's years, almost all of whom, including the villains, were prepared to share their knowledge with me and guide me into the paths of angling, if not moral righteousness. Where did I read, I wonder, that someone (John Buchan, I think) had once remarked of Tiberius, a man whose life began well and ended ignobly, that no fisherman can be wholly vile? I tried to look this up, since I like the sentiment, but I failed to confirm the elusive memory of it, and until it comes back

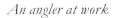

An angler at work

to me, you must take it on trust and accept it as a truth proven by my experience. Take my word for it: somewhere below the red, irascible face of the most violent angler, interrupted in mid-cast by an innocent bystander and moved to express himself somewhat floridly, lies a sweet-natured, upstanding Christian gentleman, honourable in every regard and much loved by all who know him.

Or so I choose to think, since it is a generous assessment, which most anglers would naturally endorse. But is it true? Does standing about on a cold river bank really help to tame the latent savagery in our bucolic breasts? Are fishermen different from other sportsmen; gentler perhaps, and more philosophical; less inclined to shout foul and blame others for their shortcomings? Do we act more decently in our business lives, and beat our wives rather less than most men? If so, there would be a strong case for prescribing fishing as a means of rehabilitating criminals. Except, of course, poachers. 'Six months on the Test, without the option' (except for Scots, who could choose the Dee) might be a reasonable sentence for shady city men, or hard-nosed handbag snatchers. Surely such offenders would come out into the new season dawn as changed men, pledged to no sin more venial than telling an occasional fib about the size of their catches.

The idea of fishing as remedial therapy is not entirely fanciful. It repairs the ravaged minds of business tycoons and massages away the high-powered tensions of the great and the good. Indubitably—a word writers use when they have no basis for their claims other than prejudice—fishing does tend to foster a certain philosophic approach to life and to nourish in its followers an ability to greet all triumphs and disasters with aplomb. If team sports make administrators capable of running other people's lives, then fishing makes men capable of running their own—a challenge which is often beyond the reach of those most prone to advising their fellows.

When I first began as a bailiff, I suppose I would have said that the main threat to the future of river fishing was large-scale, illegal netting on the estuaries. A decade later, I am not so sure. Now, everyone holds to a different view as to which of several serious threats to fish and fishing outweighs all others. But there is general agreement that the following, which I deliberately list in no particular order, are matters for concern.

(1) The pressure of increasing numbers of people on limited river space, and on the land surrounding rivers.

(2) Pollution in all its forms, but most notably (in rural areas) farm slurry, pesticides, and the discharge of sewage.

(3) Poaching, particularly the netting of fish on the estuaries.

(4) Fish farming, and the stocking of rivers with varieties of alien fish.

(5) Excessive water abstraction.

(6) The run-off of nitrates from highly fertilized fields.

Dry fly

Doubtless, there are other causes for disquiet, and I have listed only those threats to our future that are the common currency of most angling discussion. I know that not all of them are of equal concern in every part of the country; water abstraction and the run-off of nitrates, for example, affect Dartmoor rivers far less than the chalk streams of Hampshire and Wiltshire, and to that extent, Devonians might be inclined to forget how damaging they can be. But I would argue that pollution is indivisible. Anglers should regard the problems of other anglers as their own, for sooner or later there is a good chance that they will be faced with the same threats.

I suspect, however, that the prospect of anglers joining together in happy harmony is a somewhat distant one. Dry-fly men find it hard enough to talk to those who favour the wet; river men look down on those who use lakes; game fishermen cross the road if they see coarse anglers on the same pavement, and sea-fishermen would never think of marrying the sister of a dedicated salmon enthusiast. I exaggerate, but not by too much. Perhaps all of us in our various forms must begin to speak with one voice if we wish the fisherman's case to be heard above the noisy lobbies of the developers and the road men. I repeat: what affects my river this week may affect your lake next; the stream which supports trout

may be part of the same river system that supports chubb and perch. None of us can afford to remain indifferent to the woes of the other.

Acting together; forming a lobby; making use of a potentially heavy voting clout is not something to which anglers are much disposed. In the past, sport fishermen have devoted remarkably little attention to the possibilities of concerted 'political' (with a small 'p') action in support of their interests, yet it is only through such action that most interests get heard. Perhaps cynicism, or simply a feeling that elections and parties and prime ministers are much less important than the serious business of fishing, has kept us aloof from everyday affairs. And despite the numbers who pursue it, angling in any form has never attracted the same media attention as other sports, nor received as many column inches of press space. Only when some poisonous discharge kills off hundreds of river fish do we get even close to the front page.

This is understandable. Angling is not a spectator sport nor one which is ever going to impinge much on the public consciousness. We go about our business quietly. We do not actively seek to expand our numbers (indeed most anglers would be happy to see them decline), and among the most expert of our practitioners we have no professional prima donnas who attract headlines—even Lady Chatterley's lover was a gamekeeper, not a water bailiff. In all essentials, we are a quiet lot, modest by temperament and middle-brow by taste. Angling (unlike hunting) was never a particularly gentlemanly pursuit until, in the form of fly-fishing, it engaged the attention of Royalty in the nineteenth century. Since then it has attracted a wider following, while remaining overwhelmingly an amateur sport, undefiled by money. The most gifted of ghillies, well versed in every aspect of salmon fishing's esoteric art, would never earn more than a twentieth of the salary of a professional football star, and televised fishing would never attract the mass audience enjoyed by snooker, or tennis.

River fishing is also not a sport which can expand indefinitely to meet new demands. Other pastimes like squash and sailing have grown immeasurably over the past thirty years without percep-tible hiccups, since sports halls and marinas can be built to order. But the facilities for river fishing cannot grow very much, since the potential venues are finite, and sooner rather than later, all the high-class English and Welsh river space will be used up, reserved for companies or the very rich. Scottish rivers may not be far behind. Already, a day's salmon fishing on some of them costs more than many people earn in a month.

This is one simple reason—there are many others—why we cannot afford to lose even the most minor of fishing rivers to pollution, water abstraction or anything else. We need to conserve what rivers we have, because what we have is very limited in

OPPOSITE
Detail of a peregrine head

relation to the population which it is meant to serve. And the same applies to fish stocks. The pressures which local poaching and large-scale ocean fishing have imposed on salmon and sea trout runs over the past twenty years must be eased, and urgently, if both species are not to disappear from this country.

Here in the South West, we face few of the problems caused by heavy industry and dense populations which require large water abstractions. Our rivers are relatively unpolluted, and our main worries are discharges of farm slurry and large-scale poaching on the estuaries, both of which could be stopped relatively easily, given the will and the money. There are already signs that heavier penalties and firmer prosecutions of farm discharges are working, since nothing engages the average farmer's attention more deeply than threats to his pocket. I am also reasonably confident that we could stop large-scale poaching on the estuaries simply by one or two additional bailiffs, whom I believe would make an impact out of all proportion to their cost.

Other problems, however, may prove more intractable, since they involve trends and developments over which we have no control. Every year, the population of the South West increases, as does the number of tourists. In the summer months, the weekend woods near Grenofen and Double Waters, midway between the market town of Tavistock and the spreading suburbs of Plymouth, are nowadays crowded with picnickers and dog-walkers. Children splash about on inflatable dinghies in the Walkham and the Tavy, while others build dams and encourage their pets to retrieve sticks. Further east, both branches of the Dart are subject to the same increasing numbers of high-spirited and innocent pleasure seekers, and few feeder streams now escape the inquisitive attentions of small boys determined to disturb whatever fish life can be found in them. As many as eighty or more cars are sometimes parked near Grenofen Bridge, where the pool is as popular a place for resting salmon going upstream as it is a target into which children can drop stones. From here, the car owners noisily spread out along both banks, seeking space in which to paddle or play football. And where the higher reaches of rivers such as the Tavy and the Dart are easily accessible, and more people find out where they are and how they can be reached, they

OPPOSITE

A 'greenback' under Grenofen Bridge in winter

too are being similarly and very rudely disturbed. Until a few years ago, the upper parts of these rivers were visited only by a few village children. Now, they are a regular rendezvous for Sunday trippers.

What effect will all these boisterous and curious humans and their dogs have on river life? Even if one assumes (and it is a sanguine assumption) that they will all carry away their litter, I cannot believe that their presence will not affect the progress of salmon towards the spawning grounds, nor the welfare of upstream trout. As more and more children come to carry it away by the pailful, the wealth of marine life which not so long ago filled West Country beaches and rock pools has now diminished considerably. Will the same happen to our rivers? Will harrassed hen fish be able to cope with all these noisy family groups? Can trout and salmon fishers exist happily on the same river used by those intent on more extrovert pleasures?

I have seen pictures of weekend fishing on the outskirts of what was once Saigon. Round a man-made pond less than half the size of a football pitch, people sit a few yards apart, casting for I am not sure what, perhaps stocked carp or telapia, happy to spend their tropical Sunday mornings at this crowded fishing fest. Could this ever catch on here, I wonder? I hardly think so. The odds must be something over a million to one against a dry-fly man ever wishing to welcome a hundred noisy others to share his beat. But someday, he may have to. The once near-perfect tranquillity of the Walkham and Tavy Valleys near Double Waters is increasingly subject to the sound of transistors from groups arriving from upstream, near Horrabridge and downstream from below Buckland. Soon, the tide of Sunday pleasure seekers must inevitably overwhelm the bird-song.

Short of employing an army of energetic wardens, I don't know how the visitors can be controlled. These particular woods are owned by a private estate which allows anyone to walk in them, and lets the fishing to a local fishing club, which in turn sells rights and tickets to the public. There is therefore little income to support the policing needed to keep the river unsullied by the clamorous throng of pleasure seekers. Short of a miracle, I see no hope that the perverse British will ever desist from claiming their

OPPOSITE
A moorland brownie

Robin Armstrong

own space in quiet beauty spots, and then proceeding to wreck the quiet in loud appreciation of Radio One. I also see little sign that people are paying much attention to anti-litter campaigns. From personal knowledge over several years of patrolling here, the biggest concession they make to tidiness is to put their rubbish in a plastic bag which is then left, neatly tied and discreetly hidden under a bush, where the foxes are not meant to ravage it. The foxes, I fear, always do.

As time goes on, the future of the Walkham and the Tavy as fishing rivers begins to look less assured. Only a few miles away from a Plymouth which is rapidly growing outwards, it may be hard to stop some future demand that the once quiet woods be taken over for 'leisure development'. After all, there are many more people who simply want to escape the city and mess about among the greenery, complete with bats, balls, buckets, spades and an overpowering urge to splash about in running water, than there are fishermen and nature-watchers. And who, as I have mused elsewhere, is to deny them, even if their demands will come to mean an end to fishing on traditional trout streams?

Most Britons, and bailiffs are no exceptions, share an aversion to crossing bridges before we come to them, preferring to tackle problems only when they cannot be escaped. So I doubt if anyone will ever sit down and consider where fishing might be in twenty years from now. But the questions, to which I certainly don't know the answers, are already presenting themselves. How will the rights be owned and who will take up the duties which go with them? How can the claims of different and usually conflicting interests in our rivers be resolved? What will be the role of the National Rivers Authority in sorting out these claims?

Perhaps I am naïve, or ignorant. Perhaps these matters are already being considered by people more expert than I am. Perhaps, indeed, I exaggerate the extent of the problems which I believe are likely to arise. Perhaps, and more importantly, it is presumptious to raise these issues when this book is meant to be a simple account of a bailiff's typical year, not a treatise on social policy?

Let me therefore leave the realms of conjecture and revert to reality. Now I am no longer a bailiff, weighed down with official concerns and responsibilities, I can take my pleasures more lightly. I have the freedom to fish whenever I want and wherever I have the right permissions and permits. Though my present trade still takes me along the river bank, photographing birds and fish to be captured in later paintings, I can now choose where I walk and how long I stay out. I can say 'Good Morning' to my erstwhile colleagues and wish them well as they prepare for a long slog up the Cherrybrook, or lay the groundwork for an evening expedition against 'lampers' at Denham Bridge, knowing smugly that I do not have to go with them. I have no regrets. Although part of me misses the friendships and fulfilments (and the financial security) of my old job, there are compensations in being self-employed. I no longer have to worry about unexpected call-outs, or court appearances, or plodding through cold mud. I no longer have to bend a humble knee to anyone unworthy, nor to put up with aggression from people who are living off crime and my

A raven cawing loudly

Field sketch of salmon on spawning beds

taxes. And I no longer need distress myself about policies with which I disagree.

When I began as a bailiff, I could look forward to running my own 'patch', the area encompassing the Tavy and the Walkham Rivers, from estuary to their separate sources in the hills above the Tavistock-Ashburton Road. Within that area, I began to know all the places and people important to my work. I began to know the pools and the redds and overhangs; I began to know the regular poachers and the riparian owners from whom they were poaching. I began to know the flora and the fauna and the ways of the rivers. I began to know as much as anyone can know about the well-being of the fish for which I was responsible. I was the governor of my small but important bailiwick, charged with the negative duty of policing my rivers and the positive one of improving the fishing in them. It was my own small business, and if things went wrong, the fault was mine.

Sadly, in my view, the expansion of the recreation and fisheries branch of the old Water Authority meant that changes in the old system became almost inevitable. Specialists were appointed in different areas. The bailiff, who was already multi-functional within his own 'patch' became so over a wider area. One night we would be on the Tavy, the next on the Tamar, miles away. Some pre-planned anti-poaching patrols would be organized from headquarters, without my knowledge. A special man was charged with farm inspections (against potential slurry discharges) when in the old days, I would have maintained such farm liaisons myself, thus helping to build up local relationships and finding our own solutions to local problems.

In short, I was encouraged to look after my own district, with help, if I needed it, on call from headquarters. It was a system which encouraged local pride and local loyalties, and certainly made the bailiff feel less like a cog in a large and faceless machine. No doubt the management experts had their own good reasons for change, and perhaps the organization which they designed was, in theory, more efficient. But uniforms turned us into officials rather than fishermen's friends, and the reallocation of duties from headquarters meant a huge loss of personal contact with those who owned the river rights and the many others who used the rivers. The changes were not to my liking, and I never felt comfortable with them. A bailiff, I think, should be seen as part of the public world of fishing who is there to help, not as part of officialdom who is there to chide.

But that is over. My full-time business now is to paint and to write and to dream up new projects which will pay the bills. I rejoice in it, even if it does sometimes demand rather more self-discipline than comes to me naturally. Painting professionally is not easy. I can discipline myself to tackle small sketches even when I don't feel much like doing them, but a large-scale painting is a different matter, calling for inspiration in addition to hard work. And even when the inspiration comes, I need to be relaxed and in

Bedstraw hawk moth

the right mood if I am to paint at all well. Thus when I parted from the old Water Authority in circumstances which caused me to fret, I left several commissions unfulfilled, although I desperately needed the money from them, simply because I lacked the emotional serenity to complete them.

Happily, I am now back on an even keel, and painting has again become a pleasure which rarely palls. Though I mostly, and repeatedly paint birds and fish, I never get bored with them. Every painting is new. Every fish and every bird is different, and each one presents different problems in the way I put it down on paper. Most of my chosen subjects are usually moving about in air or water, and I have to work from memory, or sketches and photographs. But I can never keep away from the river for very long without losing the feel for what I am trying to depict. I may be working in a studio, but the need to see a real fish, or a real bird rather than a photograph is ever pressing. If I'm painting a heron, however many I've seen in the past, I need to see one again, in the flesh—if I simply drew one from an old photograph, I should never be satisfied with it. To infuse life and a sense of wonder into any painting, I need to keep close to the things I paint.

And so, given my chosen subjects, I cannot see myself easily giving up my country way of life. I might be persuaded to leave Devon, for there is hardly a single part of the British Isles which hasn't some marvellous natural scenery to offer, but I wouldn't easily forego living far away from a good fishing river. Even those many years spent as a bailiff, tackling all the day-to-day chores which go with that job, have not diminished my pleasure in being 'on the water', preferably a trout water and on a good day, with the right rod and tackle and the prospect of a good pint ahead. The pleasure of it never diminishes, and nor do my hopes for further similar pleasures to come. I reckon any man lucky who is able to fish, and doubly lucky if he has a small talent to draw. If Armstrong as bailiff is ended, Armstrong as full-time artist is only just beginning.

Discarded bird's feather